The ESSENTIALS® of
REGISTERED TRADEMARK

ENGLISH LANGUAGE

Mamie Webb Hixon, M.A.

Director of the Writing Center
University of West Florida
Pensacola, Florida

Research and Education Association
61 Ethel Road West
Piscataway, New Jersey 08854

THE ESSENTIALS®
OF ENGLISH LANGUAGE

REVISED PRINTING 1997

Printed in the United States of America

Library of Congress Catalog Card Number 95-78966

International Standard Book Number 0-87891-789-6

ESSENTIALS is a registered trademark of
Research & Education Association, Piscataway, New Jersey 08854

WHAT "THE ESSENTIALS" WILL DO FOR YOU

This book is a review and study guide. It is comprehensive and it is concise.

It helps in preparing for exams, in doing homework, and remains a handy reference source at all times.

It condenses the vast amount of detail characteristic of the subject matter and summarizes the **essentials** of the field.

It will thus save hours of study and preparation time.

The book provides quick access to the important principles, grammar, and structures in the language.

Materials needed for exams can be reviewed in summary form – eliminating the need to read and reread many pages of textbook and class notes. The summaries will even tend to bring detail to mind that had been previously read or noted.

This "ESSENTIALS" book has been prepared by an expert in the field, and has been carefully reviewed to assure accuracy and maximum usefulness.

Dr. Max Fogiel
Program Director

CONTENTS

CHAPTER 1

The Noun

A *noun* is a part of speech that names a person, place, thing, idea, animal, quality, or action. Along with verbs, nouns are the principal elements of any sentence.

Into each *life* some *rain* must fall.

On his *vacation* in *California, Jason* called his *sister.*

John gave the *men* their *money* for the *work.*

All the italicized words in the above sentences are examples of nouns. Just as people can be classified according to a number of characteristics, such as hair color, height, weight, occupation, income, or nationality, so can nouns be classified according to specific characteristics.

1.1   Proper and Common Nouns

Most nouns are *common nouns.* They name any one of a class or kind of people, places, or things. A *proper noun* is the official name of a particular person, place, or thing. The writer's main problem with proper nouns is recognizing them so they can be capitalized (see **Capitalization**).

Proper nouns include the following:

1.1.1 Personal names

Mr. William Jones	Susan Lee Gray
Dr. Harrison	Captain Smith
John Mills, Jr.	Mrs. Laurence
Zeus	St. Francis
Pope Paul	President Roosevelt

1.1.2 Names of Nationalities and Religions

Frenchman	Judaism
Englishman	Catholicism
Mexican	Christianity

1.1.3 Geographic Names

Paris	Seine River
New York City	England
Peking	Mount Wilson

1.1.4 Names of Holidays

Christmas	Rosh Hashanah
Columbus Day	Thanksgiving Day

1.1.5 Names of Time Units

Monday	February

1.2 Concrete and Abstract Nouns

A noun that names a member of a class, a group of people, places, or things is a *concrete noun,* because what it names is physical, visible, and tangible. *Abstract nouns* name a quality or a mental concept, something intangible that exists only in our mind. Compare:

CONCRETE NOUNS	ABSTRACT NOUNS
book	truth
rose	beauty

1.3   Collective Nouns

A noun used to describe a group of people or things that is considered a single unit is called a *collective noun*. Some examples are

orchestra	family	band
herd	flock	chorus
committee	audience	gang
Congress	crowd	multitude
faculty	staff	personnel
crew	team	group
government	press	bunch
class	nation	
majority	jury	

1.4   Countable and Noncountable Nouns

Most nouns can be made plural by changing the ending (usually by adding "s"). These are called *countable nouns*. There is a group of nouns, however, that have no plural. These are called *noncountable nouns,* because the members of the group they represent are either singular or plural depending on the context. Two main groups of noncountable nouns are

1.4.1   Mass Nouns

cheese	moss	coffee
dust	wine	measles

These are nouns that describe concrete objects considered in a mass quantity.

1.4.2   Abstract Nouns

courage	fun	mathematics

Occasionally, some of these nouns take a plural form if a variance of the object described is stressed.

How many *cheeses* (different kinds) did you taste?

That store carries more *teas* (kinds of) than any I've seen.

1.5   Noun Compounds

A *compound* is a group of words (usually two) that functions as a single part of speech.

Her *mother-in-law* watched closely as the *blackbirds* fluttered about the *birdbath* behind the *flower garden*.

That *store clerk* had no *common sense*; he took the *traveler's check* without even checking the signature on a *credit card*.

Noun compounds generally take one of the following forms:

1.5.1   Noun and Noun

birdbath   credit card
bookstore   author-editor

1.5.2   Adjective and Noun

blackbird   common sense

1.5.3   Possessive Noun and Noun

traveler's check   citizens' committee

1.5.4   Noun and Prepositional Phrase

mother-in-law   editor in chief

1.5.5   Noun, Conjunction, and Noun

trial and error   breaking and entering

1.5.6   Verb and Noun

search warrant   stoplight

1.5.7   Gerund and Noun

firing squad   managing editor

1.5.8 Noun and Verb

handclasp   ice skate

1.5.9 Preposition and Noun

downpour   afterthought

1.5.10 Noun and Gerund

problem solving   decision making

1.5.11 Verb and Adverbial Preposition

break-in   cleanup

1.6 Gender

In English there are four genders. They are not indicated by inflective forms but by entirely different words.

MASCULINE	FEMININE	COMMON (either sex)	NEUTER (no sex)
father	mother	parent	marriage

1.7 Number—Plural Nouns

Most nouns can be singular or plural. The usual plural form adds "s" to the end of the word.

desk	desks	book	books

However, there are exceptions to this guideline. After a "y" preceded by a consonant, the "y" changes to "i" and "es" is added.

sky	skies	secretary	secretaries

If the final "y" is preceded by a vowel, no change is made, and the plural is formed by adding "s."

decoy	decoys	attorney	attorneys

If the last sound in the word is "s," "z," "ch," "sh," or "x," then "es" is added so that the word can be easily pronounced.

class	classes	branch	branches

However, if the "ch" is pronounced "k," only "s" is added.

stomach	stomachs

Often the final "fe" or "f" in one-syllable words becomes "ves."

half	halves
wife	wives

There are exceptions, of course.

chief	chiefs
roof	roofs

Many nouns have plural forms that are irregular.

child	children	mouse	mice
woman	women	series	series

For nouns ending in "o," add "s" or "es" to form the plural. These spellings must be memorized individually.

potato, potatoes	hero, heroes

Finally, there are a number of foreign words that have become part of the language and retain their foreign plural form. There is a trend to anglicize the spelling of some of these plural forms by adding "s" to the singular noun. In the list that follows, the letter(s) in parentheses indicate the second acceptable spelling as listed by *Webster's New Collegiate Dictionary*.

datum	data
medium	media
crisis	crises
parenthesis	parentheses
criterion	criteria
phenomenon	phenomena (s)

As you can see, there are many peculiarities associated with plural formation. It is advisable to have a dictionary on hand to check plural forms.

1.8 The Possessive Case

The possessive case of singular nouns and some singular indefinite pronouns is formed by adding an apostrophe and "s."

a fox's cunning	the mother's hope
the girl's dress	anyone's choice
Mr. Smith's hopes	New Year's Day

Also, add an apostrophe and "s" to singular nouns that end with an "s" or an "s" or a "z" sound, unless the sound is unpleasant or difficult to pronounce. Some writers use only the apostrophe for singular nouns that end with an "s" or an "s" or a "z" sound.

> the witness's testimony
> Dickens's story OR Dickens' story

Unpleasant sound:

> Ulysses's travels   Moses's beliefs

The possessive case of plural nouns ending in "s" is formed by adding only an apostrophe.

the foxes' cunning	the mothers' hope
the girls' dresses	the Roberts' address

The possessive case of plural nouns not ending in "s" is formed by adding an apostrophe and an "s."

the children's game	the men's store
the people's court	women's liberation

Errors to Avoid

Do not use the possessive case of a noun when the plural form is needed.

NO	*YES*
keeping up with the Joneses'	keeping up with the Joneses
the Kennedys'	the Kennedys
men's	men

Some words, phrases, and expressions contain a fixed apostrophe:

> for goodness' sake

7

bachelor's degree, bachelor's degrees
collector's item, collector's items

Sometimes the possessive case is not necessary:

family support group	humanities scholar
teacher salaries	AIDS victims

1.8.1 The "Of" Phrase

When the possessive form refers to an animate object, such as a person, the addition of apostrophe or apostrophe "s" to the noun is the standard procedure. However, an "of" phrase is most often preferred when the possession refers to an inanimate object. Therefore, we write

the color of the cup	*NOT* the cup's color
the lines of the paper	*NOT* the paper's lines

Inanimate things do not possess. Unfortunately, this guideline has its own exceptions. There are many occasions when we use the possessive form to indicate possession for nouns referring to things.

The following are some exceptions:

EXPRESSIONS OF TIME

the year's end	a day's work
three weeks' pay	today's weather

NATURE

the tree's roots	the moon's phases

MONEY OR MEASURE

a dollar's worth	an arm's length

GROUPS OF PEOPLE

the newspaper's headlines	the restaurant's employees

There is no clear rule. Besides the idioms mentioned, there are numerous others that appear to violate even the most reliable rules.

the book's success	the policy's failure

The "of" phrase is sometimes used with nouns referring to animate objects, especially to modify a long or awkward construction and to avoid a piling up of possessives.

NO: The dog's collar's latch was broken.

YES: The latch of the dog's collar was broken.

Any name consisting of several words that would be awkward in the possessive also uses the "of" phrase.

NO: The director of the Health, Education and Welfare Department's message to the president...

YES: The message of the director of the Health, Education and Welfare Department to the president...

Always try to keep the reader or the listener in mind; use the construction that will convey your meaning most clearly.

1.8.2 Possessives in a Series

When one of the words in a series is a possessive, all of the other words in that series must also be in the possessive case.

NO: Bill, Henry, George, and my new restaurant...

YES: Bill's, Henry's, George's, and my new restaurant...

1.8.3 Joint Possession—Different Possession

Joint possession is also used when each word in a series possesses something different.

NO: James and Michael's paintings are similar.

YES: James' and Michael's paintings are similar.

NO: The chefs and chauffeurs' uniforms continue to last.

YES: The chefs' and chauffeurs' uniforms continue to last.

1.8.4 Joint Possession—Similar Possession

When each word in a possessive series owns the same thing, the possessive is formed on the last word only.

NO: Let's go over to John's and Mary's house. (If you made "house" plural, you would be visiting two houses.)

YES: Let's go over to John and Mary's house.

1.8.5 Possession With Gerunds

A *gerund* looks like a verb but is used as a noun. It is the "ing" form of the verb. The participle looks like a gerund because it also ends in "ing," but it serves as an adjective, not as a noun. (See **Verbals** for further explanation of these terms.)

When a noun or a pronoun immediately precedes a gerund, it is usually possessive.

His arriving when he did pleased us all.

The *senators'* voting was divided.

However, if the word preceding the gerund is an inanimate object, we use the "of " phrase, because it is usually agreed that inanimate objects do not possess.

NO: The car's starting delighted Susan.

YES: The starting of the car delighted Susan.

1.8.6 Parallel Possession

In parallel structure, parallel ideas are expressed in the same grammatical form. Therefore, in parallel construction, the possessive form is carried through.

NO: His life is more burdensome than his wife.

YES: His life is more burdensome than his wife's.

1.8.7 Possessive Followed by an Appositive

When a possessive is followed by an *appositive* (a word or group of words complementing or supplementing another), apostrophe "s" is added to the appositive.

It was Jason the gardener's move.

An appositive (or explanatory word or group of words) set off by commas implies that it is not essential to the meaning of the sentence. In such a case, the possessive may be formed on both the main noun and the explanatory word or on only the explanatory word.

10

It was Jason's, the gardener's, move.

or

It was Jason, the gardener's, move.

1.8.8   Possession With Compound Words

Use the last word in a compound word to form the possessive even if the compound is not hyphenated.

SINGULAR POSSESSIVE	*PLURAL*	*PLURAL POSSESSIVE*
mother-in-law's	mothers-in-law	mothers-in-law's
commander in chief's	commanders in chief	commanders in chief's

1.8.9   Double Possessive

A double possessive, perfectly acceptable in English, uses both apostrophe "s" and an "of " form.

friends of Mary's   relatives of Mr. Green's

CHAPTER 2

Pronouns

Pronouns are the simple, everyday words used to refer to the people, places, or things that have already been mentioned, such as *him, she, me,* and *it,* or to indefinite people, places, things, or qualities, such as *who, where, this,* and *somebody.* Pronouns usually replace some noun and make an expression concise. There are only about 50 pronouns in the English language, and most of them are short words; however, they can be difficult to use correctly. One reason these words may be so difficult to use properly is their frequency of occurrence. Of the 25 most commonly used words in the English language, ten are pronouns. Perhaps it is due to their frequent usage that pronouns have acquired a variety of distinctive functions. Although pronouns are used in different ways, they have two things in common. The first is their ability to stand alone, or "stand in" for nouns. The second is that they all have little specific meaning. Whatever meaning they have derives from the context in which they are found. Some pronouns that modify other words are also adjectives. This chapter will speak mainly of pronouns that stand alone—that take the place either of a definite noun or of an unknown or uncertain noun. Pronouns used as adjectives are discussed in the chapter **Adjectives and Adverbs.** Pronouns used as adjectives in examples in this chapter are marked (a.).

Whom are *you* speaking to?

That is *my* (a.) hat *you* are holding in *your* (a.) hand.

12

Marsha *herself* told *them all* (a.) about *what* happened to *her* when it started to rain.

Somebody had to let the *others* know *that she* was not to blame.

Who, what, where, when, and *how* are the five words by which *you* can organize this.

This is a new kind of information for *me,* and *I* regret to *some* (a.) degree *that I* can't be more in touch with *them.*

All the italicized words in the preceding sentences are pronouns. Traditionally, pronouns are divided into six groups; each group has its own name, definition, and special functions. These categories are helpful in learning how to recognize the different kinds of pronouns and how to use them correctly, since they come in such a wide variety of forms.

2.1 Types of Pronouns

2.1.1 Personal Pronouns

Because of their many forms, these can be a troublesome words.

CASE

Number	Person		Subject	Object	Possessive	Possessive Adjective
Singular	First		*I*	*me*	*mine*	*my*
	Second		*you*	*you*	*yours*	*your*
	Third*	(masc.)	*he*	*him*	*his*	*his*
		(fem.)	*she*	*her*	*hers*	*her*
		(neuter)	*it*	*it*		*its*
Plural	First		*we*	*us*	*ours*	*our*
	Second		*you*	*you*	*yours*	*your*
	Third		*they*	*them*	*theirs*	*their*

Subject: _____ *saw it.* Object: *Let* _____ . Possessive: *That's* _____ .
Possessive Adjective: _____ *house.*

* When a pronoun is used to refer to someone (other than the speaker or the person spoken to), the third person is used, and a different form of the pronoun is employed to show the gender of the person referred to. *His, her, him, his,* and *hers* all indicate the masculine or feminine gender. *It* and *its* refer to something to which gender does not apply.

There are three forms of personal pronouns.

13

PERSON: to indicate whether the person is the speaker (first person), the person being spoken to (second person), or the person being spoken about (third person).

CASE: to show the job the pronoun is performing in the sentence.

NUMBER: to indicate whether the word is plural or singular.

Examples of Personal Pronoun Use

I went yesterday to see *her.*

Between *you* and *me, I* really don't want to go with *him.*

Errors to Avoid—Pronoun Case

When a compound subject or object includes a pronoun, be sure that the case chosen is in agreement with the pronoun's place in the sentence: a subject case pronoun is used as the subject of the verb, an object case pronoun is used as the object, etc. The same rule of agreement is true when using an appositive (a word or words with the same meaning as the pronoun); the pronoun must be in the same case form as the word it renames.

Compounds

Both Mary and he (NOT him) have seen that movie.
(subject—"Mary and he")

Last year the team elected both Jane and me (NOT I).
(object—"Jane and me")

Could you wait for my brother and me (NOT I)?
(object of a preposition—"my brother and me")

It was I (NOT me) who received the award.
(subject complement—"I")

Appositions

We (NOT us) Americans value freedom. *(subject)*

Let's you and me (NOT I) go together. *(object)*

Our school sent two delegates, Mark and him (NOT he). *(object)*

It is not for us (NOT we) writers to determine editorial policy. *(object)*

2.1.2 Relative Pronouns—Interior Sentences (Clauses)

Relative pronouns play the part of subject or object in sentences within sentences (clauses). They often refer to nouns that have preceded them, making the sentence more compact.

NO: The flower—the flower was yellow—made her smile.

YES: The flower, *which* was yellow, made her smile.

NO: The girl—the girl lived down the block—loved him.

YES: The girl *who* lived down the block loved him.

Sometimes their reference is indefinite.

I wonder *what* happened. (The event that occurred is uncertain.)

I'll call *whomever* you want. (The people to be called are unknown.)

Who (for persons), *that* (for persons and things), *where* (for places), and *which* (for things) are the most common pronouns of this type.

2.1.3 Interrogative Pronouns—Questions

These pronouns are easy to recognize because they always introduce either direct or indirect questions. The words just discussed as relative pronouns are called *interrogative* pronouns when they introduce a question: *who, what, which, whom, whose, whoever, whichever,* and *whatever.*

Who is at the door? (refers to a person)

What do you want from me? (refers to a thing)

Which (flavor) do you want? (refers to a thing)

Which (a.) boy won the match? (refers to a person)

Whatever you mean by "liberal education," I don't know.

Whom did you telephone last night?

Sometimes these relative pronouns introduce subordinate (dependent) clauses.

She wondered *who* was at the door.

Samuel asked them *what* they wanted.

He didn't know if he would ever find out *what* happened.

I couldn't guess *which* they would choose.

2.1.4 Demonstrative Pronouns—Pointers

This, that, these, and *those* are the most common words used as pronouns to point to someone or something clearly expressed or implied.

That is the apple I wanted. (subject)

Bring me *those*, please. (object)

I must tell him *that*. (object)

These are the ones I've been looking for. (subject)

"*This* above all, to thine own self be true." (subject)

Such and *so* may also serve as pointing pronouns:

Such was his fate. (subject)

He resented Jerry and told him *so*. (object)

These same words are often used as adjectives, and at first glance it is easy to classify them only as adjectives, forgetting that they also take the place of nouns and serve as pronouns.

That apple is the one I want. (adjective describing "apple")

Bring me *those* books, please. (adjective describing "books")

2.1.5 Reciprocal Pronouns

The reciprocal pronouns are *each other* and *one another*. *Each other* is preferred when the reference is two nouns, and *one another* is preferred when the reference is more than two nouns.

Romeo and Juliet love *each other*.

The members of the fraternity support *one another*.

2.1.6   Reflexive Pronouns

These are the pronouns that end in "self" or "selves."

myself	yourself	yourselves
himself	herself	itself
ourselves	themselves	

Their main purpose is to reflect back on the subject of a sentence.

She cut *herself.* (object, refers to "she")

I bought *myself* a new dress. (object, refers to "I")

They consider *themselves* lucky. (object, refers to "they")

2.1.7   Intensive Pronouns

Reflexive pronouns also provide emphasis. When they serve this purpose, they are used to intensify the meaning of the noun or pronoun they accompany.

We will triumph over this outrage *ourselves.*

I will go to the ticket office *myself.*

She will tell it to him *herself.*

Errors to Avoid—Reflexive Pronouns
Do not use the reflexive in place of the shorter personal pronoun.

NO: Both Sandy and *myself* plan to go.

YES: Both Sandy and *I* plan to go.

Watch out for careless use of the pronoun form.

NO: George *hisself* told me it was true.

YES: George *himself* told me it was true.

NO: They washed the car *theirselves.*

YES: They washed the car *themselves.*

Notice that the reflexive pronouns are not set off by commas.

NO: Mary, *herself,* gave him the diploma.

YES: Mary *herself* gave him the diploma.

2.1.8   Indefinite Pronouns

This group of pronouns acquired its name because the reference (the noun for which they are standing in) is indefinite.

Indefinite persons or things (all singular pronouns)

each	everything
either	something
one	anything
neither	nothing
everybody	everyone
somebody	someone
anybody	anyone
nobody	no one
other	

Everybody joined in the chorus.

No one took less than he did.

Is *anyone* here?

I hope *someone* answers my calls.

Indefinite quantities

one	neither	none
each	much	either
another	all	some
several	both	few
least	less	little
lots	many	plenty
other	most	more

Much has been said on the subject of delinquency.

Many are called, but few are chosen.

Each must chart his own course.

The following pronouns are plural:

several
few
both
many

These pronouns may be singular or plural, depending on the use:

    all
    some
    most
    none
    any
    more

Some of the mail *has* arrived.
Some of the letters *have* arrived.

2.2 Case—The Function of the Pronoun in a Sentence

By far the pronouns with which we are apt to make the most mistakes are those that change their form when they play different parts in a sentence—the personal pronouns and the relative pronoun *who*. A careful study of the peculiarities of these changes is necessary in order to avoid the mistakes associated with their use.

2.2.1 Subject Case (Used Mainly When the Pronoun is a Subject)

Use the *subject case* (*I, we, you, he, she, it, they, who,* and *whoever*) for the following purposes:

1.   As a subject or a repeated subject

    NO: Mrs. Jones and *me* left early yesterday.

    YES: Mrs. Jones and *I* left early yesterday. (subject of "left")

    NO: I know *whom* that is.

    YES: I know *who* that is. (subject complement of "is")

    NO: *Us* girls always go out together.

    YES: *We* girls always go out together. ("we" is the subject; "girls" repeats it)

2. Following the verb "to be" when it has a subject

This is a part of the language that appears to be changing. It is a good example of how the grammar of a language follows speech and not the other way around. The traditional guideline has been that a pronoun following a form of "be" must be in the same case as the word before the verb.

It is *I*. ("It" is the subject; *I* is the subject complement.)

I thought it was *she*. ("It" is the subject; *she* is the subject complement.)

Was it *they* who arrived late? ("It" is the subject; *they* is the subject complement.)

Our ear tells us that in informal conversation, "It is I" would sound too formal, so instead we tend to say

It is *me*. (in conversation)

I thought it was *her*. (in conversation)

Was it *them* who arrived late? (in conversation)

In written English, however, it is best to follow the standard of using the subject case after the verb "be" when "be" is preceded by a word in the subject case, even though the pronoun is in the position of an object.

Here are some more examples that might cause trouble.

NO: Last week the best students were *you* and *me*.

YES: Last week, the best students were *you* and *I*. (refers to "students," subject of "were")

NO: Whenever I hear that knock, I know it must be *him*.

YES: Whenever I hear that knock, I know it must be *he*. (refers to "it," subject of "must be")

3. As a subject when the verb is omitted (often after *than* or *as*)

I have known her longer than *he*. ("has known her" is elliptical)

She sings as well as *I*. ("sing" is elliptical)

We do just as well in algebra as *they*. ("do" is elliptical)

20

He is much better than *I* at such calculations. ("than I am at such calculations"——"am" is elliptical)

To test whether the subject or the object form is correct, complete the phrase in your mind and it will be obvious.

Often a relative pronoun like *that, which, who, whom,* or *whoever* will act as the subject of a clause.

Tell me *who* was singing.

Arnold knew something *that* was generally unknown.

Do you remember *which* kind is better?

Give it to *whoever* has the most need.

2.2.2 Object Case (Used Mainly When the Pronoun is an Object)

Use the *object case (me, us, him, her, it, you, them, whom, whomever)* as follows:

1. As the direct or indirect object, object of a preposition, or repeated object

The postman gave *me* the letter. (indirect object)

Mr. Boone appointed *him* and *me* to clean the room. ("him and me" are the objects of "appointed" and the subject of the infinitive "to clean")

They told *us* managers to rewrite the first report. ("us" is the indirect object of "told"; "managers" repeats)

Between *you* and *me*, I'm voting Republican. (object of "between")

Whom were you thinking about? (object of "about")

2. As the subject of an infinitive verb

Janet invited *him and me* to attend the conference.

3. As an object when the verb or preposition is omitted

Father told my sister June more about it than (he told) *me*.

The telephone calls were more often for Marilyn than (they were for) *him*.

4. Following "to be"

In point number 2, it was shown that the subject of an infinitive verb form must be in the object case. The infinitive "to be" is an exception to this rule. Forms of "to be" must have the same case before and after the verb. If the word preceding the verb is in the subject case, the pronoun following must be in the subject case also. (For example, It is *I*.) If the word before the verb is an object, the pronoun following must be objective as well.

We thought the *author* of the note to be *her*.

You expected the *winner* to be *me*.

5. Subject of a progressive verb form that functions as an adjective (participle—"ing" ending)

Two kinds of words commonly end in "ing": a *participle,* or a word that looks like a verb but acts like an adjective, and a *gerund,* a word that looks like a verb but acts like a noun. When an "ing" word acts like an adjective, its subject is in the object case.

Can you imagine *him acting* that way? ("Acting" refers to the pronoun and is therefore a participle, which takes a subject in the object case, "him.")

They watched *me smiling* at all the visitors. ("Smiling" refers to the pronoun, which must be objective, "me.")

Compare:

Can you imagine *his acting* in that part? (Here the emphasis is on "acting"; "his" refers to "acting," which is functioning as a noun—it is a gerund—and takes the possessive case.)

It was *my smiling* that won the contest. (Emphasis is on "smiling"—it is playing the part of a noun and so takes a possessive case pronoun, "my.")

2.2.3 Possessive Case

Use the *possessive adjective case (my, our, your, her, his, its, their, whose)* in the following situations:

1. To indicate possession, classification of something, or connection. Possession is the most common.

22

I borrowed *her* car. (The car belongs to her.)

Come over to *our* house. (The house belongs to us.)

The plant needs water; *its* leaves are fading.

2. Preceding a verb acting as a noun (gerund)

Our leaving early helped end the party.

Whose testifying will you believe?

Since there are no possessive forms for the demonstrative pronouns *that, this, these,* and *those,* they do not change form before a gerund.

> NO: What are the chances of *that's* being painted today?
>
> YES: What are the chances of *that* being painted today?

Use the *possessive case (mine, ours, yours, hers, his, its, theirs, whose)* in any role a noun might play—a subject, an object, or a complement with a possessive meaning.

Hers was an exciting career. ("Hers" is the subject of "was.")

Can you tell me *whose* this is? ("Whose" is the complement of "is.")

He is a friend of *mine*. ("Mine" is the object of the preposition "of.")

We borrowed *theirs* last week; it is only right that they should use *ours* this week. ("Theirs" is the object of the verb "borrowed"; "ours" is the object of the verb "use.")

2.3   *Who* and *Whom*

Who is a subject case pronoun. It may be used as the subject or subject complement of an independent or a subordinate clause.

Who are you? ("Who" is the subject complement; it refers to the subject "you.")

We were not sure *who her next opponent would be.* (In this subordinate clause, "who" is the subject complement referring to "opponent," the subject of the clause.)

He is a person *who* we think *is very qualified for the position*. (In this subordinate clause, "who" is the subject of "is.")

He is the person *who was selected for the job*. (In this subordinate clause, "who" is the subject of "was selected.")

Whom is an object case pronoun. It may be used as a direct object, indirect object, or object of a preposition in an independent or a subordinate clause.

Whom would you like to speak to? ("Whom" is the object of the preposition "to.")

Whom did you call? ("Whom" is the object of the transitive verb "did call.")

We were not sure *for whom the bell tolled*. (In this subordinate clause, "whom" is the object of the preposition "for.")

Voters elected a candidate *whom they could trust*. (In this subordinate clause, "whom" is the direct object of the transitive verb "could trust.")

2.4   *Whoever* and *Whomever*

Whoever is a subject case pronoun. It may be used as the subject or subject complement of a subordinate clause.

Give the ticket to *whoever wins*. (In this subordinate/noun clause, "whoever" is the subject of the verb "wins"; the entire clause is the object of the preposition "to.")

Give the ticket to *whoever the winner is*. (In this subordinate/noun clause, "whoever" is the subject complement referring to "the winner"; the entire clause is the object of the preposition "to.")

Whomever is an object case pronoun. It may be used as an object in a subordinate clause.

Give the ticket to *whomever the committee recommends*. (In this subordinate clause, "whomever" is the direct object of the transitive verb "recommends"; the entire clause is the object of the preposition "to.")

2.5 Agreement

A pronoun usually takes the place of some noun. The noun (or group of words that works as a noun) for which the pronoun stands in is called the *antecedent*. It usually comes before the pronoun in the sentence or the paragraph. It is important to remember that the pronoun and the word(s) it refers to have to agree. If the antecedent is plural, the pronoun must be plural; if the antecedent is singular, the pronoun must also be. The gender and person must also be consistent.

The *woman* raised *her* hand.

The *children* raised *their* hands.

2.5.1 Number

Number refers to whether a pronoun is singular or plural. A singular pronoun should be used with a singular antecedent:

Every dog has *its* day.

A plural pronoun should be used with a plural antecedent:

All pet owners must feed *their* pets.

2.5.2 Gender

Gender refers to whether a pronoun is masculine, feminine, or neuter.

The woman has *her* share of problems. (feminine)

The man has *his* share of problems. (masculine)

The country has *its* share of problems. (neuter)

2.6 Reference of Pronouns

2.6.1 Ambiguous Pronouns

Can you make sense out of the following paragraph?

Harry called to David while he was coming down the stairs. David told Harry that he should not talk for long since he had laryngitis. Harry said that it wouldn't take long. Then he told David that he had seen him raking leaves. He said that he made a big mistake. David asked what he had done wrong.

Harry replied that everyone could see where he made his mistake that looked closely.

Try it now.

Harry was coming downstairs when he called out to David. David said, "I can't talk very long; I have laryngitis." Harry replied, "This won't take long. I saw you when I was raking leaves, and I want to tell you that you made a big mistake." David asked, "What did I do wrong?" Harry replied, "Anyone who looked closely could see what you did wrong."

Pronouns can add grace and variety to our writing. Yet they become a problem when we use them too much or when it is difficult to tell exactly what or whom the pronoun is referring to. This is the most important lesson to learn about pronouns: make sure that it is clear what the pronoun is referring to.

> NO: It was dark and it was heavy, and I tripped over it and dropped it down the stairs.

> YES: It was dark, and the box was heavy. I tripped over something and dropped the box down the stairs.

> NO: When Mary saw Anne, she told her that she would be happy to help her with the project.

> YES: When Mary saw Anne, Anne told her that she would be happy to help Mary with the project.

> NO: He was late, but he didn't know it.

> YES: He was late, but Andy didn't know it.

Who and *which* and *that* can create similar problems. Make sure that it is clear what each pronoun refers to.

> NO: Tom said he saw a cute little monkey who usually doesn't care about animals.

> YES: Tom, who usually doesn't care about animals, said he saw a cute little monkey.

> NO: He charged so high a price for the job that is generally considered unethical.

YES: He charged so high a price for the job that it is generally considered unethical.

NO: My father is quite famous as a chemist, which I know nothing about.

YES: My father is quite famous as a chemist, but I know nothing about chemistry.

When readers see a pronoun, they look for a nearby noun to determine what the pronoun stands for. If the noun is too far away, readers have to hunt for it. This slows down and irritates readers.

NO: I shut the door and concentrated only on my work. It was old and heavy and shut out every sound.

YES: I had to concentrate on my work, so I shut my door. It's old and heavy, and it keeps out every sound.

2.6.2 Use of *That* and *Which*

The use of *that* and *which* often presents a problem for the writer. The difference is simple: If the clause is essential to the meaning of the sentence, use *that*. If the clause is not essential to the meaning of the sentence, use *which,* and set off the clause with commas.

THAT: The book that contained the formula was missing. *(It is essential that the formula be in the missing book.)*

WHICH: The book, which contained the formula, was missing. *(It is essential only that the book is missing.)*

CHAPTER 3

Expletives

Dictionaries say that *it* and *there* are pronouns, but actually they are somewhat different from pronouns. They have even less meaning than the sometimes vague or indefinite pronouns. Because they provide so little information, their sole function is to fill space and to provide a formal subject for a sentence.

3.1   It

3.1.1   *It*—Impersonal and *It*—Real Subject

When *it* introduces sentences about the weather, time, or date, it is the real subject. *It* is also the real subject when it substitutes for a noun.

It's cold outside. (what is "it"?)

It's March 3.

What is this? *It*'s my comb.

It's ten after three.

It's a twenty-minute walk to the grocery store.

It seems warmer than yesterday.

I know *it* gets crowded here at noon.

3.1.2   *It*—Anticipatory

Sometimes *it* fills the subject position, while the actual subject appears later in the sentence. The nonitalicized sections of the following sentences are the actual subjects:

It's surprising how handsome he is.

It's interesting to know your background.

It's curious that Mary paints so well.

It's good knowing you are waiting for me.

3.2   There

3.2.1   *There* as an Expletive

Notice how *there* has no meaning but only fills the space of the subject.

In these sentences, *there* is not the real subject, it is an expletive.

There are three of us watching you.

There is lightning outside.

There are many ways to peel an onion.

There's a sale at Sears.

3.2.2   *There* as an Adverb

There is also often used as an adverb. If *there* is an expletive (a space filler), it is likely to be accompanied by "a." If it is accompanied by "the," it is probably an adverb and not a space filler.

There she is…Miss America.

There in the middle of the highway was a bag full of money.

There she goes.

There is the money on the table.

CHAPTER 4

Verbs

Every sentence must have a verb. *Verbs* express action or a state of being. Small changes in their form reflect many differences in meaning. One variable is number; a verb can be either singular or plural.

I *am* happy to be here. (singular)
We *are* not so sure of the date. (plural)

Jill *loves* chocolate chip cookies. (singular)
Mother and father *love* to go sailing. (plural)

Verbs are also distinguished by person: first (I, we), second (you), and third (he, she, it, one, they). Usually, verbs change form only in the third person singular.

I, you, we, they *hope* you will stay.
He, she *hopes* you will leave.

Changes made in the forms of words in order to indicate slight changes of meaning are called *inflections.* Verbs change more readily and more often than any other sort of word; this can be confusing. By hearing English spoken and by learning to speak it yourself, you have probably learned the rules and peculiarities associated with correct verb usage without even thinking about it; you know that when something "sounds right," it probably is. But there are rules and logic to explain why some things sound right and others don't. When something sounds wrong to your ear, it is probably due to a mistake in either tense, irregular verb usage, or agreement.

4.1 Kinds of Verbs

4.1.1 Transitive Verbs and Objects

Verbs can express action. The subject is the one who does the action. The noun that receives the action is the *object.*

Harold studied *physics.*

Charles invited *Mary and David.*

This machine cleans *carpets.*

When a verb takes an object to complete its meaning, it is called a *transitive verb.* A transitive verb usually needs an object to make sense.

NO: The company built.

YES: The company built an alarm into the system.

NO: Ellen and Harry thanked.

YES: Ellen and Harry thanked their lucky stars.

NO: We all make.

YES: We all make our own breakfast.

Sometimes transitive verbs can do without an object, as in: *Harold studied* or *This machine cleans.* However, they usually take an object.

A noun or pronoun is called the *direct object* when it is the direct receiver of the action of the verb, as in the examples above. The *indirect object* is the noun or pronoun that tells us *to whom* or *for whom* the action was done. In the following examples, the italicized words are indirect objects.

Did they leave *us* any cake? (Did they leave any cake for *us?*)

Are you talking to *me?*

Alan bought *Susan* a racing bike. (Alan bought a racing bike for *Susan.*)

If the preposition *to* or *for* is present in the sentence, then the noun or pronoun for whom or to whom the action is done is the object of the preposition, not the indirect object.

31

Michael wrote a song for *Daphne*.

Did you give the key to *Jennifer*?

4.1.2   Intransitive Verbs and Complements

Intransitive verbs are verbs that do not take an object. They can stand alone with the subject.

The sun also *rises*.

Babies must *crawl* before they can *walk*.

Intransitive verbs often use complements to complete their meaning. Complements are quite different from objects. They do not receive the action of the verb, but they complete its meaning.

The sun rises *early*.

The baby can crawl *quite quickly.*.

Notice that the complements in the above examples are an adverb or an adverbial (a word or group of words that acts like an adverb). Intransitive verbs use adverbs as complements. Copulative verbs can use adjectives as complements, but intransitive verbs cannot.

NO: The baby can crawl so *quick!*

YES: The baby can crawl so *quickly!*

NO: He moved *cautious.*

YES: He moved *cautiously.*

4.1.3   Copulative or Linking Verbs and Complements— Sensing Verbs

A verb describes either an action or a state of being. Transitive and intransitive verbs describe actions. *Copulative verbs* describe only states of being. The verb *to be* is the most common copulative verb. Others are *act, appear, seem, become, remain, look, sound, feel, smell, taste,* and *grow.*

The complement of a copulative verb refers to the subject. It modifies or completes the meaning of the subject.

The complement of a copulative verb may be a noun:

Ben Jonson was a *contemporary* of Shakespeare.

Moby Dick is a complex *book.*

a nominal (a word or group of words that acts like a noun):

His argument was *that man is a rational creature.*

or an adjective:

His head feels *cool.*

Copulative verbs always take an adjective for a complement rather than an adverb. This may sometimes sound funny, but it makes better sense.

Compare

Sensing Verb	*Intransitive Verb*
The radiator felt cool.	Ralph behaved coolly.
Some fruits are quite bitter.	A spoiled child was crying bitterly.

Linking verbs occasionally take adverbials as complements, particularly adverbials of time or place.

The professor is *in his office.*

The plane is *on the runway.*

Linking Verbs:

be	shall be	should be
being	will be	would be
am	has been	can be
is	have been	could be
are	had been	should have been
was	shall have been	would have been
were	will have been	could have been

Verbs of the Senses:

appear	grow	seem	stay
become	look	smell	taste
feel	remain	sound	turn

4.1.4 Auxiliaries

has	can	might
have	may	must
had	should	do
shall	would	
did	could	
will		
does		
is		

All forms of the verb *be* are auxiliaries when they accompany a main verb, for instance, *is leaving* and *was going*.

4.2 Forms of the English Verb

With the exception of *be* which has eight forms, every English verb, whether regular or irregular, has five forms:

	REGULAR	*IRREGULAR*
the base form	walk	go
the -*s* form	walks	goes
the -*ing* form	walking	going
the -*ed*/past form	walked	went
the participle form	walked	gone

4.3 Tense

Tense relates to time. Verbs have the ability to tell us not only what action is occurring but also when it is occurring. The form of a verb changes in order to indicate when an action takes place. The two main forms of any verb are the present and the past tense. The past tense is usually formed by adding "ed" to the basic verb.

PRESENT	*PAST*
walk	walked
listen	listened
enter	entered

Verbs that follow this pattern in forming the past tense are called regular verbs. Almost all of the verbs in the language are regular. Yet, there are about 100 commonly used verbs that do not follow this pattern. These are known as irregular verbs and will be discussed in more detail later in the chapter.

Although the past and present are the only form changes in single-word verbs, there are certain verb phrases that are also used with the verbs to indicate changes in time. When these verb phrases are added to the past and present tenses, there are actually six tenses in the English language.

Present:	present time, action or condition going on now (*yawn, am yawning*).
Past:	past time, action is completed (*yawned*).
Future:	future time, action or condition is expected to happen or come (*will yawn, shall yawn*).
Present Perfect:	action occurred in the past and is complete in the present (*have* or *has yawned*).
Past Perfect:	past action completed before another past action (*had yawned*).
Future Perfect:	future action to be completed before another future action (*will have yawned*).

As you can see, some of these tenses make it possible to express quite subtle variations in time. The three perfect tenses as well as the future tense are formed by adding a helping, or auxiliary, verb to the past participle, which is usually formed by adding "ed" to the main verb. The perfect tenses show that an action has been completed (perfected).

All six of the main tenses also have a companion form: the progressive form. This can also be considered a tense, as it shows that action is in progress. Progressive forms are expressed with some form of the verb *to be* and the ending "ing" added to the main verb. Examples:

He *is looking* at the birds. (present progressive)

They *were looking* at the mirror. (past progressive)

He *will be looking* for her tomorrow. (future progressive)

I *have been looking* at the tree. (present perfect progressive)

We *had been looking* for a house. (past perfect progressive)

She *will have been looking* for the right material for her drapes for three years. (future perfect progressive)

It is not necessary to learn the names of all these tenses; they are introduced only so that you may gain some familiarity with the terms and a better understanding of the logic behind the language. The most important parts of the study of verb forms for an English-speaking student are both the study of common errors and practice in using the correct forms.

The verbs that are apt to cause the most trouble are the irregular verbs, because it is easy to confuse the past tense and the past participle.

He drank (NOT drunk) his fill of beer.

After he had eaten (NOT ate) his dinner, he left.

I had gone (NOT went) down to see Jim.

He began (NOT begun) his day early.

To review, the regular verbs form the past tense by adding "d" or "ed" to the present tense of the verb. The irregular verbs form the past tense in a number of different ways; there are no rules governing the formation of the past tense and the past participles. They have to be studied and learned. Review the list of commonly used irregular verbs in section 4.4.1 to find the ones that most often cause you trouble.

Errors to Avoid in Tense of Verbs

Do not use the present for the past tense.

      NO: Yesterday, he *sees* her twice.

      YES: Yesterday, he *saw* her twice.

Do not use the present for the future tense.

      NO: Tomorrow I *drive* into town.

      YES: Tomorrow I *shall drive* into town.

Do not use the past for the past perfect tense.

NO: John asked whether I *ate* all my dinner.

YES: John asked whether I *had eaten* all my dinner.

Do not shift from the present to the past in the same phrase.

NO: The boy *is raking* the leaves and *went* for the basket.

YES: The boy *is raking* the leaves and *goes* for the basket.

Do not shift from the past to the present in the same phrase.

NO: She *sat* at the window and *looks* out.

YES: She *sat* at the window and *looked* out.

4.4 Regular and Irregular Verbs

4.4.1 Main Parts of Commonly Used Irregular Verbs

PRESENT TENSE	PAST TENSE	PAST PARTICIPLE
am	was	been
arise	arose	arisen
awake	awoke, awaked	awaked, awoken
bear	bore	borne
beat	beat	beaten
become	became	become
begin	began	begun
bend	bent	bent
bind	bound	bound
bite	bit	bitten
bleed	bled	bled
blow	blew	blown
break	broke	broken
bring	brought	brought
broadcast	broadcast, broadcasted	broadcast, broadcasted
build	built	built
burn	burned, burnt	burned, burnt
burst	burst	burst
buy	bought	bought

PRESENT TENSE	PAST TENSE	PAST PARTICIPLE
cast	cast	cast
choose	chose	chosen
cling	clung	clung
come	came	come
cost	cost	cost
creep	crept	crept
deal	dealt	dealt
dig	dug	dug
dive	dived, dove	dived
do	did	done
*drag	dragged	dragged
draw	drew	drawn
dream	dreamed, dreamt	dreamed, dreamt
drink	drank	drunk
drive	drove	driven
*drown	drowned	drowned
eat	ate	eaten
fall	fell	fallen
feed	fed	fed
fight	fought	fought
find	found	found
flee	fled	fled
fling	flung	flung
*flow	flowed	flowed
fly	flew	flown
forget	forgot	forgotten
forgive	forgave	forgiven
freeze	froze	frozen
get	got	got, gotten
give	gave	given
go	went	gone
grind	ground	ground
grow	grew	grown
hang (a picture)	hung	hung
hang (a person)	hanged	hanged
hear	heard	heard

PRESENT TENSE	PAST TENSE	PAST PARTICIPLE
*heat	heated	heated
hide	hid	hidden
hit	hit	hit
hold	held	held
hurt	hurt	hurt
kneel	knelt	knelt
know	knew	known
lay (to place)	laid	laid
lead	led	led
leap	leaped, leapt	leaped, leapt
leave	left	left
lend	lent	lent
let	let	let
lie (to rest)	lay	lain
lie (to tell a lie)	lied	lied
light	lighted, lit	lighted, lit
lose	lost	lost
make	made	made
mean	meant	meant
meet	met	met
mistake	mistook	mistaken
pay	paid	paid
prove	proved	proved, proven
put	put	put
*raise	raised	raised
read	read	read
rid	rid	rid
ride	rode	ridden
ring	rang	rung
rise	rose	risen
run	ran	run
say	said	said
see	saw	seen
seek	sought	sought
sell	sold	sold
send	sent	sent

PRESENT TENSE	PAST TENSE	PAST PARTICIPLE
set	set	set
sew	sewed	sewn, sewed
shake	shook	shaken
shine (glow; gleam)	shone, shined	shone, shined
shine (polish)	shined	shined
show	showed	shown, showed
shrink	shrank	shrunk
sing	sang	sung
sink	sank, sunk	sunk
sit	sat	sat
slay	slew	slain
sleep	slept	slept
slide	slid	slid
sling	slung	slung
slink	slunk	slunk
sow	sowed	sowed, sown
speak	spoke	spoken
speed	speeded, sped	speeded, sped
spell	spelled, spelt	spelled, spelt
spend	spent	spent
spit	spit, spat	spit, spat
spring	sprang	sprung
stand	stood	stood
steal	stole	stolen
stick	stuck	stuck
sting	stung	stung
stink	stank, stunk	stunk
strike	struck	struck
strive	strove, strived	striven, strived
swear	swore	sworn
sweat	sweated, sweat	sweated, sweat
sweep	swept	swept
swim	swam	swum
swing	swung	swung
take	took	taken
teach	taught	taught

PRESENT TENSE	*PAST TENSE*	*PAST PARTICIPLE*
tear	tore	torn
tell	told	told
throw	threw	thrown
thrust	thrust	thrust
understand	understood	understood
wake	woke, waked	woken, waked
wear	wore	worn
weave	wove, weaved	woven, weaved
weep	wept	wept
win	won	won
wind	wound	wound
wring	wrung	wrung
write	wrote	written

*Not an irregular verb but past forms are often misused (*drug* for the past form of *drag*, for instance).

Errors to Avoid in Principal Parts of Verbs

Do not confuse the past participle with the past tense.

> NO: I *swum* two miles last week.
>
> YES: I *swam* two miles last week.
>
> NO: My shirt *shrunk* in the wash.
>
> YES: My shirt *shrank* in the wash.

Learn the irregular verbs. Do not add regular endings to irregular verb stems.

> NO: She *arised* late on Tuesday.
>
> YES: She *arose* late on Tuesday.
>
> NO: The batter *swinged* at the ball.
>
> YES: The batter *swung* at the ball.

Do not confuse the past tense with the past participle. Only the past participle uses helping verbs.

> NO: He must have already *broke* the door.
>
> YES: He must have already *broken* the door.

NO: They had *began* early.

YES: They had *begun* early.

4.4.2 *Lie* and *Lay* and Other Troublesome Verbs

Do not confuse similar verbs. Two pairs of verbs that often cause trouble are *lie* and *lay* and *sit* and *set*.

PRESENT	*PAST*	*PAST PARTICIPLE*	*"ING" FORM*
Lie (to rest)	lay	lain	lying
Lay (to place)	laid	laid	laying
Sit (to be seated)	sat	sat	sitting
Set (to place)	set	set	setting

Lay and *set* are transitive and always take an object because they refer to something. *Lie* and *sit* are intransitive and stand alone.

NO: *Lay* down here and rest.

YES: *Lie* down here and rest.

NO: The pen is *laying* on the table.

YES: The pen is *lying* on the table.

NO: I had *laid* down for a nap.

YES: I had *lain* down for a nap.

NO: The dog was *setting* there.

YES: The dog was *sitting* there.

NO: She *sat* it down on the floor.

YES: She *set* it down on the floor.

4.5 Agreement Between Subjects and Verbs

When parts of a sentence agree, there is a logical relationship between them. The most important kind of agreement is between the subject and the verb. The verb must agree with the subject in both number and person. That is, if the subject is singular, the verb must also be; if the subject is plural, the verb must be plural. If the subject is in the third person (he, she, it, one, they), the verb must also be in the third person. The main difficulty is identifying the subject of the sentence and determining whether it is singular or plural. (For discussions of how to recognize singular and plural subjects, see **The Noun** and **Pronouns**.)

4.5.1 Subjects Followed by Additives

Do not be distracted by words that come between the subject and the verb. Remember to always make the verb agree with the subject of the sentence.

NO: The *arrival* of many friends *promise* good times.

YES: The *arrival* of many friends *promises* good times.

NO: *All* the Democrats, including John, *hopes* Murray wins.

YES: *All* the Democrats, including John, *hope* Murray wins.

NO: Every *one* of you *know* your subject well.

YES: Every *one* of you *knows* your subject well.

4.5.2 Subjects That Follow Verbs

In sentences in which the subject follows the verb, be especially careful to determine the subject and make it agree with the verb.

NO: In the back of the room *sits* many of my *friends*.

YES: In the back of the room *sit* many of my *friends*.

NO: Into the dark *stares* her black *cats*.

YES: Into the dark *stare* her black *cats*.

NO: There *is* many *pictures* on the wall.

YES: There *are* many *pictures* on the wall.

4.5.3 Subjects Joined by Correlative Conjunctions

When singular subjects are joined by *either...or, neither...nor, or,* or *nor,* the verb is singular.

NO:	Either the *principal* or the football *coach* usually *attend* the dance.
YES:	Either the *principal* or the football *coach* usually *attends* the dance.
NO:	I'm sure that neither the *lawyer* nor the *accountant are* to blame.
YES:	I'm sure that neither the *lawyer* nor the *accountant is* to blame.

If one of the subjects is plural and one singular, make the verb agree with the subject nearest it.

NO:	Neither the *cat* nor the *dogs is* eating today.
YES:	Neither the *cat* nor the *dogs are* eating today.
NO:	Either the *students* or the *teacher speak* at any one time in this classroom.
YES:	Either the *students* or the *teacher speaks* at any one time in this classroom.

4.5.4   Words Used as Words or Titles

Remember that a word used either as a word or as the title of a particular work, even if it is plural, requires a singular verb.

NO:	*Politics are* a noun.
YES:	*Politics is* a noun.
NO:	The *New York Times print* informative, reliable stories on most subjects.
YES:	The *New York Times prints* informative, reliable stories on most subjects.

4.5.5   Other Subjects

The difficulty with collective nouns is trying to decide whether to use the singular or plural verb form. When the emphasis is on the collection, the singular is used, as in:

The *orchestra* plays at noon every day.

If the emphasis is on the individual members of the group, the plural verb is required.

The *orchestra* are unable to work well together.

Therefore, the meaning of the sentence determines which form is correct. This problem will be treated in more detail in the discussion of agreement between the subject and the verb.

Collective nouns can be used in the plural form.

The *teams* are ready to begin.

I heard both *orchestras* last night.

Subjects preceded by *each, every, many a,* and *the number of* are singular.

> NO: The number of students dropping out of school have increased.
>
> YES: The number of students dropping out of school has increased.
>
> NO: Every employee have a key to the building.
>
> YES: Every employee has a key to the building.

4.6 Verbals

Verbals are words that originate from verbs. They can be confusing because they are like verbs and, at the same time, like other parts of speech. They have verb forms: the *gerund, infinitive,* and *participle,* and, like verbs, they can show tense, take complements, and be modified by adverbs. They function, however, like other parts of speech: the *noun, adjective,* and *adverb.* In short, verbals are verb forms that do not function as verbs.

4.6.1 Gerunds

The *gerund* is a verb form that ends in "ing" and is used as a noun.

Writing a paper is not as easy as you might think.

John's *laughing* in class caused the principal to reprimand him.

The gerund has two tenses: *present* and *perfect.* (The perfect tense refers to action occurring before the action represented by the main verb in the sentence.)

> present: *walking, speaking*

> perfect: *having walked, having spoken*

Eating all those cookies gave Johnny a stomachache.

Having missed the bus made us late for the concert.

4.6.2   The Infinitive

The *infinitive* is the basic form of the verb, usually preceded by the preposition "to." It may function as a *noun,* an *adjective,* or an *adverb.*

> to write   to run

It is not as easy *to write* a paper as you might think.

To run every day requires diligence.

The infinitive also has two tense forms: present and perfect.

> present: *to walk, to speak*

> perfect: *to have walked, to have spoken*

Mary had *to walk* to the bus stop.

We were supposed *to have completed* the job by Monday.

4.6.3   The Participle

The *participle* is a verb form that usually ends in "ing" or "ed" or, less frequently, "en," "d," or "t." It functions primarily as an adjective, although it may also serve as an adverb.

The *laughing* boy was silenced by harsh words.

Frightened, the little girl hid behind her mother.

The *stolen* purse was retrieved by the police yesterday.

The participle has three tense forms: present, past, and perfect.

> Present participle: *walking, speaking*

> Past participle: *walked, spoken*

> Perfect participle: *having walked, having spoken*

The man *walking* down the street is her uncle.

The paper, *having been written* and *revised*, was ready for publication.

The table, well *constructed*, was on display at the museum.

4.7   Voice

Voice is the relationship of the subject to the verb, that is, whether the subject is the performer of the action or whether it is the receiver of the action.

4.7.1   Active Voice

An *active voice* sentence is one in which the subject is the performer of the action:

The pitcher hit the ball.

Someone stole the jewels.

4.7.2   Passive Voice

A *passive voice* sentence is one in which the doer of the action is either unknown or irrelevant; the subject is then the receiver of the action:

The ball was hit by the pitcher.

The jewels were stolen.

In general, use the *active voice* in writing. The *passive voice* should be used only when there are specific stylistic or contextual reasons.

A transitive verb is either active or passive. When the subject acts, the verb is active. Similarly, when the subject is acted upon, the verb is passive.

In writing, the active voice is preferable because it is emphatic and direct. A weak passive verb leaves the doer unknown or seemingly unimportant. However, the passive voice is essential when the action of the verb is more important than the doer, when the doer is unknown, or when the writer wishes to place the emphasis on the receiver of the action rather than on the doer.

Examples Using the active voice rather than the passive.

> Weak Passive: The garbage can was hit by the station wagon.

> Strong Active: The station wagon hit the garbage can.

Example Using the passive voice.

> Another man was hired yesterday.

Here, the action of the verb is more important than the doer.

> All the buildings were destroyed during the bombing.

In this example, the emphasis is on the receiver of the verb.

4.8   Mood

The form or the *mood* of a verb indicates something about the action. In the English language, there are three moods: the indicative, the imperative, and the subjunctive.

The Indicative Mood: The indicative mood makes a statement or poses a question.

> We are leaving.   Are we leaving?

The Imperative Mood: The imperative mood expresses a command, a request, or a direction.

> Don't touch the sculpture..

The Subjunctive Mood: The subjunctive mood is used in *that* clauses that express motion, resolution, recommendation, command, or necessity.

> I recommend that the plans be carried through.

The subjunctive mood is also used in *if* clauses that express doubt or the impossibility of the condition.

> If I had the time, I would join the tennis club.

Lastly, the subjunctive mood is used in main clauses to express hope, wish, or prayer.

> God save the queen.

The verb *to be* often gives writers difficulty. In the subjunctive mood, use the verb *to be* as follows:

    a.   *Be* in all forms of the present tense.

    b.   *Were* in all forms of the past tense.

    c.   *Have been* in all forms of the present perfect tense.

CHAPTER 5

Adjectives and Adverbs

Adjectives and adverbs always appear in relation to some other word; they are *modifiers.* They have so much in common that they can be considered together.

The opposing team played *an aggressive, sophisticated* game.

All of the words italicized above are *adjectives.* You can recognize an adjective because it always refers to a noun, a pronoun, or any other word or group of words playing the part of a noun. Adjectives qualify, describe, or limit nouns or pronouns.

The italicized words in the following sentence are *adverbs.* Adverbs refer to verbs, adjectives, or other adverbs.

She thought *deeply* about her *most dearly* loved companion, *then* left *immediately* with a *little* more hope that she could *still* find him *soon.*

As you can see, modifiers are a part of almost all sentences. Although only the subject (noun or pronoun) and the verb are necessary for a complete sentence, such a simple construction is unusual. "Time flies" is an example of such a minimal expression. Even a short sentence such as "The dog barks" contains a modifier. The more complex a sentence becomes, the more modifiers are used. Modifiers help to make the meaning of a sentence clearer and more exact. A careful study of them is important to good writing.

5.1 Recognizing Adverbs and Adjectives

Sometimes we can recognize a word as an adverb or an adjective by its form, but sometimes the same form of a word is used for both functions. In these cases, it is difficult to distinguish between an adverb and an adjective. One clue is that many adverbs end in "ly." Here is a comparison of the adjectival and adverbial forms of some nouns.

NOUN	ADJECTIVE	ADVERB
truth	truthful	truthfully
intention	intentional	intentionally
theory	theoretical	theoretically

Not all adverbs end in "ly," and to complicate matters there are a number of adjectives that do.

Examples of adverbs that do not end in "ly"

now	still	quite
then	when	almost
soon	here	very
yet	too	often

Now they are ready to be *very* helpful.

Call me *often* if you *still* love me.

Examples of adjectives that end in "ly":

lovely	orderly	timely
lively	friendly	lonely

Mary is a *lovely* girl, but her sister Jean is *homely*.

It was a *timely* decision that led to *friendly* relations between the two schools.

Some words have the same form whether they are used as an adjective or an adverb. For example:

well	deep	right
early	fast	wrong
little	late	better
very	above	hard
much	long	

The difference between adverbs and adjectives actually depends not on distinctive endings but on the way the word functions in a sentence. If the word modifies a noun, it is an adjective. If it modifies an adjective, adverb, or verb, it is an adverb.

Is he *well?* (adjective)

Does he type *well?* (adverb)

Fast though he was, he couldn't keep up with Stevens. (adjective)

How *fast* can you run? (adverb)

There are some adverbs that have two acceptable forms—one with an "ly" ending and one without the "ly" ending. Usually, the "ly," or longer, form is preferred—especially for writing. The shortened form is more likely to be used in speaking informally. Examples of these adverbs are

direct — directly	slow — slowly
tight — tightly	close — closely

Though we often drop the "ly" in speech, it is usually not correct and should be avoided.

NO: Don't talk so *loud*.

YES: Don't talk so *loudly*.

NO: You *sure* have all the luck.

YES: You *surely* have all the luck.

5.2   Degrees of Adjectives and Adverbs

Adjectives and adverbs have three forms that show a greater or lesser degree of the characteristic of the basic word: the *positive,* the *comparative,* and the *superlative.* The basic word is called the positive. The comparative is used in referring to two persons, things, or groups. The superlative is used to refer to more than two people, things, or groups; it indicates the greatest or least degree of the quality named. Most adjectives of one syllable become comparative by adding "er" to the ending; they become superlative by adding "est" to the ending. In adjectives ending with "y," the "y" changes to "i" before the endings are added.

Examples of comparison of adjectives:

POSITIVE	COMPARATIVE	SUPERLATIVE
big	bigger	biggest
happy	happier	happiest
late	later	latest
lovely	lovelier	loveliest

Adjectives of two or more syllables usually form their comparative degree by adding "more" (or "less"); they form their superlative degree by adding "most" (or "least").

Examples of comparison of adjectives of two or more syllables:

POSITIVE	COMPARATIVE	SUPERLATIVE
handsome	more handsome	most handsome
	less handsome	least handsome
timid	more timid	most timid
	less timid	least timid

Some adjectives are irregular; their comparatives and superlatives are formed by changes in the words themselves.

Examples of comparison of irregular adjectives:

POSITIVE	COMPARATIVE	SUPERLATIVE
good	better	best
many		
much	more	most
some		
bad	worse	worst
little	less	least
far	farther	farthest
	further	furthest

Def.: *Farther* refers to a greater physical distance.
Further refers to a greater degree, time, or quality.

Adverbs are compared in the same way as adjectives of more than one syllable: by adding "more" (or "less") for the comparative degree and "most" (or "least") for the superlative.

Examples of comparison of adverbs:

POSITIVE	COMPARATIVE	SUPERLATIVE
easily	more easily	most easily
	less easily	least easily
quickly	more quickly	most quickly
	less quickly	least quickly

Some adverbs are irregular; some add "er" or "est."

Examples of comparison of irregular adverbs:

POSITIVE	COMPARATIVE	SUPERLATIVE
little	less	least
well	better	best
far	farther	farthest
badly	worse	worst
fast	faster	fastest
soon	sooner	soonest
much	more	most

The comparative and superlative indicate not only the differences in the degree of the quality named, but also in the number of things discussed.

Use the comparative to compare two things.

Mary is the *lazier* of the two.

I've tasted *creamier* cheese than this.

Use the superlative to compare more than two things.

Mary is the *laziest* girl I know.

This is the *creamiest* cheese I've ever tasted.

There are some words to which comparison does not apply, because they already indicate the highest degree of a quality. Here are some examples.

Adverbs and adjectives with no comparison:

immediately	superlative	first
last	very	unique
uniquely	universally	perfect

perfectly	exact	complete
correct	dead	deadly
preferable	round	perpendicularly
square	third	supreme
totally	infinitely	immortal

Errors to Avoid in Comparison

Do not combine two superlatives.

NO: That was the *most bravest* thing he ever did.

YES: That was the *bravest* thing he ever did.

Do not combine two comparatives.

NO: Mary was *more friendlier* than Susan.

YES: Mary was *friendlier* than Susan.

5.3 Comparison with "Other" or "Else" or "Of All"

A common mistake when comparing members of a group is to forget to indicate that the item being held up for comparison is still a part of the rest of the group to which it is being compared. The addition of "other" or "else" to the comparative makes this relationship clearer. If the superlative is used, adding "of all" makes the meaning more definite and emphatic.

NO: She is a better piano player than any pianist in our group. *(Is she part of the group?)*

YES: She is a better piano player than any other pianist in our group. *(It is now clear that she is a member of the group.)*

NO: Our dog is smarter than any on the block. *(Does the dog live on the block?)*

YES: Our dog is smarter than any other on the block. *(Now it is obvious that the dog lives on the block.)*

NO: Your car is the fastest car in the neighborhood. *(Whose neighborhood?)*

YES: Your car is the fastest of all the cars in the neighborhood. *(Your car belongs in the neighborhood.)*

5.4   Confusion with Adverbs and Adjectives

5.4.1   Linking Verbs

There are two categories of verbs after which an adjectival form is used instead of an adverbial form. When using these verbs, some make the mistake of choosing an adverb instead of an adjective since, logically, the modifier seems to refer to the verb. Actually it refers to the subject.

Use an adjective after:

1.   Forms of the verb "to be" and other nonaction verbs, such as

seem	appear	become
remain	prove	

The boy was studious. *(studious boy)*

She appears happy. *(happy girl)*

2.   Verbs of the senses, such as

taste	feel	look
smell	sound	

Marianne feels sick. *(sick Marianne)*

That apple tastes good. *(good apple)*

NO: Those girls look beautifully. *(wrong)*
       Those girls are beautifully. *(illogical)*

YES: She appears happy.
       She is happy. *(logical)*

Sometimes the modifier refers to the verb, describing or clarifying the manner of the action. In this case, the adverbial form must be used.

She *felt cautiously* for the light switch. *(cautiously felt)*

Her parents *appeared immediately* after she called. *(immediately appeared)*

5.5   Faulty Comparisons

When adjectives and adverbs are used incorrectly in comparisons, the result can be illogical statements.

> NO: The crime rate in Detroit is higher. (higher than what?)

> YES: The crime rate in Detroit is higher than it is in other large cities.

> NO: The crime rate in Detroit is higher than New York. (The crime rate cannot be higher than the city.)

> YES: The crime rate in Detroit is higher than New York's.

CHAPTER 6

Prepositions

Between New York and Chicago, we came *upon* two strange signs that kept us *inside* the car *despite* our strong desire to go outside *around* daybreak. *For* hours, we stayed *on* the road contrary *to* our plan, *with* those signs reappearing *before* our eyes long *after* they had disappeared *from* our sight.

All the italicized words in the preceding paragraph are prepositions. Prepositions are connecting words; they connect the word or words that follow them (called the *object* of the preposition) with some other part of the sentence. They illustrate a relationship between words. The preposition and the word or group of words that follows it constitute the *prepositional phrase,* which can function in a sentence as an adjective, adverb, or noun.

There are two kinds of prepositions—simple, one-word prepositions and group prepositions.

6.1   Simple Prepositions

at the office	*by* the seashore	*for* your love
down south	*on* the desk	*like* her sister
through the door	*about* the house	*within* three weeks
beside the bed	*over* the top	*behind* his chair
except you	*across* town	*with* kind greetings

6.2   Group Prepositions

according to	in conjunction with	in place of
because of	as well as	in addition to
by means of	in front of	in spite of
together with	due to	along with

There are only a few rules governing the use of prepositions. Learning to use the correct preposition is really a matter of developing a good sense of what sounds right. This is acquired by listening and by trying to write the way we talk. Of course, some aspects of speech must be formalized for writing.

Errors to Avoid

In speech, there is a tendency to either overuse or omit necessary prepositions. This should be eliminated in formal writing.

Example of overuse:

> NO: Let's divide *up* the orange.

> YES: Let's divide the orange.

Example of omission:

> NO: She was concerned *about* Jamie and his many dogs.

> YES: She was concerned *about* Jamie and *about* his many dogs.

Need for different prepositions in the same phrase:

> NO: Mother was both influenced and annoyed *with* her doctor.

> YES: Mother was both influenced *by* and annoyed *with* her doctor.

Overconcern with placement:

Although in the past it was considered incorrect English to end a sentence with a preposition, it is no longer so. Current usage (everyday speech) and rhythm often necessitate putting a preposition at the end of a sentence. Excessive attention paid to following the outdated rule can result in some unnatural and confusing sentences.

> NO: Tell me *for* what you are looking.

> YES: Tell me what you are looking *for*.

6.3 Idiomatic Use Of Prepositions

Idioms are expressions that are characteristic of a particular language. The idiomatic use of prepositions has become quite popular in the English language. Here, prepositions are used after certain verbs, participles, nouns, and adjectives. New forms and meanings of these idiomatic prepositions are continually coming into the language. It is advisable to consult the dictionary to determine whether an expression is *idiomatic,* for example, "similar to," or *unidiomatic,* for example, "similar with." Other usage labels, such as informal, vulgar, and slang, should also be checked so the writer can determine whether the expression is appropriate for that particular piece of writing. The following is a brief list of some standard idiomatic prepositions. For further discussion of idioms, see **Using the Dictionary.**

abstain from	envious of
acquit of	expert in
addicted to	foreign to
adept in	hint at
adhere to	identical with
agree to (a thing)	independent of
agree with (a person)	infer from
angry at (a thing)	inseparable from
angry with (a person)	jealous of
averse to	oblivious of
capable of	prerequisite to
characteristic of	prior to
compare to (for an example)	proficient in
compare with (to illustrate a point)	profit by
concern in	prohibit from
concerned with	protest against
desire for	reason with
desirous of	regret for
devoid of	repugnant to
differ about	sensitive to
differ from (things)	separate from
differ with (a person)	substitute for
different from	superior to
disagree with	sympathize with
disdain for	tamper with
distaste for	unmindful of
empty of	

6.4 List of Common Prepositions

abaft	concerning	out of
about	contrary to	outside
above	despite	over
according to	down	past
across	during	rather than
after*	except	regarding
against	excepting	round
ahead of	for	since*
along (with)	from	through
amid	in	throughout
among	in addition to	till
anent	in back of	to
apart from	in front of	together with
around	in lieu of	toward
as*	in place of	towards
as far as	in regard to	under
as well as	in spite of	underneath
at	in view of	until*
back of	including	unto
because of	inside	up
before*	instead of	up to
behind	into	upon
below	like	versus
beneath	near	via
beside	of	with
between	off	with regard to
beyond	on	within
but	on account of	without
by	out	worth

*also used as subordinating conjunctions

CHAPTER 7

Conjunctions

Not only Susan *but also* both Andrew *and* Samuel were *either* for fighting *or* for getting out immediately, *since* no help had arrived. *Although* they all wanted to stay, the fighting was bound to begin again, *and* this time with more force *than* before.

The italicized words in the preceding paragraph are all conjunctions. Like prepositions, *conjunctions* are connecting words. They connect words, phrases, or clauses. There are four kinds of conjunctions: coordinating conjunctions, conjunctive adverbs, correlative conjunctions, and subordinating conjunctions.

7.1   Coordinating Conjunctions

Coordinating conjunctions connect parts of a sentence that are equivalent. It is fairly simple to determine whether sentence parts are equivalent: words are equal to other words; phrases are equal to phrases; main clauses are equal to main clauses; and minor (or subordinating) clauses are equal to minor clauses. The following are commonly used coordinating conjunctions:

and	but	yet	so
for	or	nor	

They may join a word to another word.

Mom *and* Dad   Jill *or* Susan   firm *yet* kind

A phrase to another phrase:

of great insight *but* of poor judgment

A minor (subordinate) clause to another minor clause:

She insisted that she knew him *yet* (that she) had not told him the story.

A main clause to another main clause:

I wanted to attend the meeting, *but* John never had the slightest intention of going.

The old grammar rule that said never start a sentence with *and* or *but* is no longer adhered to. Sometimes using a coordinating conjunction to start a sentence is very effective.

She said she would leave early. *And* she did.

7.1.1 Parallel Structures with Conjunctions

When using a coordinating conjunction, be sure that the sentence elements you are joining are equivalent.

NO: Her main interests were *that she succeed* and *skiing*.

YES: Her main interests were *success* and *skiing*.

OR

YES: Her main interests were *that she succeed* and *that she ski regularly*.

7.2 Conjunctive Adverbs

Conjunctive adverbs have a dual role. They connect independent clauses and also illustrate the relationship between the two clauses. Although the clause introduced by the conjunctive adverb is grammatically sufficient, a logical relationship exists with the other clause. Since the conjunctive adverb basically introduces a modifying clause, it is less of a connector than the coordinating conjunction.

Clauses joined by conjunctive adverbs must be separated by either a period or a semicolon. The following are some conjunctive adverbs and transitional phrases, which serve the same function.

therefore	furthermore	nevertheless
however	besides	indeed
consequently	moreover	thus
accordingly	still	hence
for this reason	likewise	on the contrary
for example	in addition	in the first place
on the other hand	at the same time	then

He won the competition in Moscow; *consequently,* he went on to have an outstanding career as a soloist.

He had shown a great deal of potential; *and for this reason,* he was given the job.

His essay provided many fine insights. *Moreover,* it was well written.

7.3   Correlative Conjunctions (used in pairs)

These conjunctions are always used in pairs that illustrate clearly that the parts they connect in a sentence are equivalent (parallel). The correlative conjunctions are

both—and	not only—but also
either—or	neither—nor
if—then	whether—or

The parts they join must be similar in form.

Either *the secretary* or *the treasurer* must preside.

Errors to Avoid

When using correlative conjunctions, a commonly made mistake is forgetting that each member of the pair must be followed by the same kind of construction.

NO: Her reaction not only *was strong* but also *immediate*.

YES: Her reaction not only *was strong* but also *was immediate*.

OR

YES: Her reaction was not only *strong* but also *immediate*.

7.4 Subordinating Conjunctions

Not all sentences are composed solely of equal parts. Usually there are some parts that are essential to the main idea and some others that serve as support or give additional information about the main idea. Subordinate conjunctions are used to help connect parts of a sentence that are unequal. Some subordinate conjunctions are

*as	because	as though	even though
*since	although	though	till
provided that	*after	*before	whenever
in order that	when	while	wherever
*until	if	unless	whereas
how	so that	that	as soon as
where	as if	as long as	

Typically, these words introduce descriptive (subordinate) clauses and connect them to the main clauses. For example:

I'll go with you *provided that* you drive.

Because she ran quickly, she arrived on time.

Faulty coordination can also be corrected by placing ideas of lesser importance in a subordinate position.

NO: He did not practice driving, *and* he failed his road test.

YES: *Because* he did not practice driving, he failed his road test.

NO: The election returns came in Tuesday night *and* weren't published in the morning paper.

YES: *Although* the election returns came in Tuesday night, they weren't published in the morning paper.

7.4.1 Relative Pronouns Used As Subordinating Conjunctions

Relative pronouns may also be used to introduce subordinate clauses: *who, whom, which, where, that.*

Other Errors to Avoid

Improper use of *while:*

While refers to time and should not be used as a substitute for *although, and,* or *but.*

> NO: *While* I'm usually interested in Fellini movies, I'd rather not go tonight.

> YES: *Although* I'm usually interested in Fellini movies, I'd rather not go tonight.

CHAPTER 8

Parts of the Sentence

A *sentence* is a group of words that makes sense, ending with a period, exclamation point, or question mark. It is the basic unit of communication. Every sentence, unless it is a command, has a subject and a predicate.

8.1   Subject and Predicate

SUBJECT	PREDICATE
Harry	drives his father's truck.
We	saw a flock of geese.
Elephants	never forget.

The *subject* is the topic of the sentence. It announces what the sentence is about. The *predicate* is what is said about the subject. The subject is generally a noun or pronoun, as in the examples above. Sometimes gerunds, infinitives, phrases, and clauses can also act as the subject. When they do, they are called *nominals* (a word or group of words that acts like a noun).

His singing woke the whole house.

What we don't know is his age.

To fly has always been man's dream.

Commands have no apparent subject. Due to the nature of the command, it is tacitly understood to be *you.*

Run as fast as you can!

Add up these numbers and tell me the answer.

Jeff, please buy me a newspaper. (Jeff is the person addressed, not the subject.)

Compound subjects are two or more simple subjects connected by *and* or *or.*

Music and dancing followed dinner.

Check or money order must accompany each application.

The *complete subject* is the simple subject and all its modifiers.

The women who sang at the party left on the 5:00 train.

A few Cadillacs were parked outside the building.

The predicate always contains a verb. The *simple predicate* is the verb without any modifiers.

Gail *laughed.*

The gorillas *bellowed.*

Edgar Allan Poe *wrote* some rather grim stories.

A *compound predicate* is two simple predicates connected by *and* or *or.*

The audience *shouted and clapped* when the curtain fell.

You either *saw* the film *or heard* about it.

8.2   Sentence Order

Usually the parts of the sentence appear in this order:

> *SUBJECT–VERB–DIRECT OBJECT*
> James   smokes   cigars.
> Bill   collects   lizards.

If there is an indirect object, it appears in front of the direct object:

SUBJECT–VERB–INDIRECT OBJECT–DIRECT OBJECT
  Harry   saved   me   some chicken.

If the verb is intransitive or copulative, (linking), the order is

SUBJECT–VERB–COMPLEMENT
Marie laughs excessively.
George is a good businessman.

Of course, sentences do not always have words in this order. Commands, for example, have no subject.

VERB–OBJECT
Drive the car.
Milk the cow.

The order of parts may be altered in a question. The example below gives the question in SUBJECT–VERB–DIRECT OBJECT order, then shows a few alternatives.

Plato wrote *The Republic?*

Did Plato write *The Republic?*

(VERB–SUBJECT–OBJECT)

Was *The Republic* written by Plato?

(VERB–Subject–COMPLEMENT)

The use of expletives will also change word order. *It* and *there,* when used as introductory words, are *expletives.* They fill the space of the subject, but an expletive is never the actual subject of a sentence.

There are bears in the woods nearby.

(VERB–SUBJECT–COMPLEMENT)

It is good for brothers to live in peace.

(VERB–COMPLEMENT–SUBJECT)

Word order is also changed for emphasis:

We cleaned the house quickly. *(normal order)*

The house we cleaned quickly. *(emphasis on "the object house")*

Birds and airplanes were in the sky. *(normal order)*

In the sky were birds and airplanes. *(emphasis on the phrase "in the sky")*

We crept to the window quietly, like thieves. *(normal order)*

Quietly, like thieves, to the window we crept. *(emphasis on how we were creeping)*

These changes in word order, especially the last example—for emphasis—add variety and color to writing.

CHAPTER 9

Phrases

"So young a child," said the gentleman *sitting opposite to her* (he was dressed *in white paper*), "ought to know which way she's going, even if she doesn't know her own name! "

A Goat that was sitting *next to the gentleman in white* shut his eyes and said *in a loud voice,* "She ought to know her way *to the ticket-office,* even if she doesn't know her alphabet! "

—Lewis Carroll, *Through the Looking Glass*

All the italicized groups of words are phrases. Phrases fill in many of the details that make a sentence interesting. For example, the sentence *"We sat."* could turn into any of the following by the addition of phrases:

We sat for hours, looking at the painting.

On the cliffs by the sea we sat, watching the sunset.

We sat by Amelia at the restaurant.

9.1   Prepositional Phrases

A *phrase* is a group of connected words without a subject or predicate. A *prepositional phrase* begins with a preposition and contains a noun and its modifiers. Some examples are

Take me *to the opera.*

The noun in a prepositional phrase is called the *object of the preposition.*

A prepositional phrase can be used as an adjective:

The woman *on the phone* is Jane.

an adverb:

A large rabbit dove *under the ground.*

or a noun:

In the evening is as good a time as any.

9.2 Gerund Phrases

A *gerund phrase* contains a gerund and its modifiers. It is always used as a noun.

Reading blueprints is not as easy as it sounds. (gerund phrase as subject)

Thoreau placed great value on *living simply.* (gerund phrase as object of the preposition *on*)

Having missed the bus, we arrived at the party late. (participial phrase as modifier)

Exercising regularly is *seizing an opportunity to keep healthy.* (gerund phrase as subject and as predicate nominative)

9.3 Infinitive Phrases

An *infinitive phrase* contains an infinitive and its modifiers. It can also be used as a noun, an adjective, or an adverb.

A waiter's job is *to serve a table.* (noun)

Tom brought a book *to lend me.* (adjective)

We'll have to run *to catch the train.* (adverb)

No one had time *to complete the extra-credit problem.* (infinitive phrase used as an adjective modifying the noun *time)*

We left early *to arrive on time.* (infinitive phrase as an adverb, modifying the verb *left)*

We hope *to win the race.* (infinitive phrase as object of verb)

The *present infinitive* also expresses the future time.

We hope *now* to win the race *in the future.*

9.4 Participial Phrases

A *participial phrase* contains a participle and its modifiers. It is used as an adjective to modify a noun or a pronoun.

The gentleman *standing in the aisle* is the owner.

Walking the balance beam, she was extremely careful. (The participial phrase modifies *she. Balance beam* is the direct object of the participle *walking.)*

Running into the house, Mary tripped on the rug. *(Running into the house* is the participial phrase. But the prepositional phrase *into the house* is also a part. It modifies the participle *running.* The participial phrase modifies *Mary. House* is the object of the preposition *into.)*

Incorrect use of a participial phrase results in a stylistic error called a *dangling participle.* For further information on such phrases, see the section **Dangling Participles.**

9.5 Absolute Phrases

An *absolute phrase* is one that is related to a sentence in meaning, though it has no grammatical relationship to the sentence. Its form is usually a noun followed by either a prepositional phrase or a participial phrase and other optional modifiers.

The reunion was planned for summer, *summer being the time of year when most people take vacations.*

The play having ended, everyone left the theater.

CHAPTER 10

Clauses

A *clause* differs from a phrase in that it has a subject and a predicate.

PHRASE: We're planning a trip *to the museum.*

CLAUSE: We're planning a trip *so that we can see the museum.*

PHRASE: *After a swim,* we'll have lunch.

CLAUSE: *After we swim,* we'll have lunch.

10.1   Independent and Subordinate Clauses

Independent/main clauses are those which can stand alone as sentences.

We lost the game. We smiled like winners.

We lost the game, but we smiled like winners.

Dependent/subordinate clauses are those which cannot stand alone as sentences. They are introduced by either a subordinating conjunction or a relative pronoun used as a subordinating conjunction. Subordinate clauses may function as adverbs, adjectives, or nouns.

An *adverb clause* functions as an adverb and usually begins with subordinating conjunctions like *as, as if, as though, than, if, until, since, before, because, after, while, when,* and *so that.*

Although we lost the game, we smiled like winners.

74

An *adjective clause* functions as an adjective and usually begins with a relative pronoun like *who, whom, whose, which, where,* or *that* (often omitted).

The game *we lost* was the semifinal in the state championship. ("that" is omitted)

The game, *which was held in the gymnasium*, generated a lot of excitement in the community.

A noun clause functions as a noun; it may serve as the subject of a sentence, the subject complement, or the object. Interrogative pronouns like *how, what, who, whom,* and *whose* usually introduce noun clauses.

What you don't know won't hurt you. (The noun clause is the subject of the sentence.)

What you see is *what you get.* (The second noun clause is the subject complement of the sentence.)

You already know *who I am.* (The noun clause is the direct object of the transitive verb "know.")

10.2   Elliptical Clauses

An *elliptical clause* is one in which words that are necessary for grammatical completeness but not for meaning are not used.

My sister is older *than I [am].*

While [I was] walking home, I met my sister.

When [you are] in Rome, do as the Romans do.

CHAPTER 11

Sentence Errors—Structural Problems

11.1 Dangling Modifiers

The dangling modifier is the most bizarre and comical of all sentence errors. Because it is such a glaring error, it stops readers dead in their tracks. The sentence lacks clarity, and the reader must take a moment to determine the writer's intention. The most common kind of dangling modifier is the dangling participle.

NO: At age six, my father taught me to swim.

YES: When I was six, my father taught me to swim.

NO: After showing the experiment, it was time to go home.

YES: After he showed us the experiment, we had to go home.

NO: The door was shut while dancing with Debbie.

YES: The door was shut while I was dancing with Debbie.

The difficulty with the sentences above is that the reader is not sure who is doing what. *"The door was shut while dancing with Debbie"* is ambiguous. *Who* is dancing with Debbie? The door? It is important to be clear about the sense of every sentence. Meaning can be completely changed when a word or phrase is moved into or out of the proper place.

Modifiers (participles, infinitives, and gerunds—verbals) usually dangle because, as in some of the examples above, the verbal is in search of a subject to modify.

11.2 Misplaced Modifiers

There are other types of modifiers that cause confusion when they are out of place. It is not important to learn the names of the various errors one could make, but it is important to avoid such errors. In general, structure a sentence logically by placing the modifier near the word it modifies. In each of the following examples, a phrase is out of place.

NO: I saw two stores and a movie theater walking down the street.

YES: Walking down the street, I saw two stores and a movie theater.

NO: Harold watched the painter gaping in astonishment.

YES: Harold watched the painter and gaped in astonishment.
Gaping in astonishment, Harold watch the painter.

NO: You can see the moon standing in the front yard.

YES: If you stand in the front yard, you can see the moon.
Standing in the front yard, you can see the moon.

There are some words that must always be placed immediately before the word they modify, or they will cause confusion. These are words like *almost, only, just, even, hardly, nearly, not,* and *merely.*

NO: Jane almost polished the plate until it shined.

YES: Jane polished the plate until it almost shined.

NO: The store on the corner only sells that toaster.

YES: Only the store on the corner sells that toaster.

Look at how the meaning can change when the modifier is moved around in the following series of sentences.

Only life exists on earth. *(There is nothing else on earth except life.)*

Life only exists on earth. *(Life does nothing but exist on earth.)*

Life exists only on earth. *(Nowhere else but on earth can one find life.)*

Life exists on earth only. *(More emphatic than the last sentence but says the same thing.)*

Place *only* and other modifiers close to the word that they modify. This is the best way to avoid ambiguity.

11.2.1 Split Infinitives

A split infinitive occurs when a modifier is placed between the sign of the infinitive "to" and the verb (*to better serve you*). In the italicized example, the infinitive "to serve" is split by the adverb "better." Careful writers try to avoid splitting infinitives.

Try to *not* split an infinitive.

The patient hopes to *fully* recover from pneumonia.

We want to *better* serve you.

11.2.2 Squinting Modifiers

A squinting modifier is one which is ambiguous because it is not clear whether it refers to the noun preceding it or the one following it.

NO: Women who like him sometimes gave him gifts.

YES: Women who like him gave him gifts sometimes.

NO: The professor sees juniors only on Fridays.

YES: The professor sees only juniors on Fridays.

11.3   Lack of Parallel Structure

When ideas are similar, they should be expressed in similar forms. When elements of a sentence are similar, they too should appear in similar form.

NO: She likes sun, the sand, and the sea.

YES: She likes the sun, the sand, and the sea.

NO: George is always singing, drumming, or he will play the guitar.

YES: George is always singing, drumming, or playing the guitar.

NO: Charlene's car skidded, turned sideways, then comes to a stop.

YES: Charlene's car skidded, turned sideways, and came to a stop.

Whenever *and* or *or* is used in a sentence, each must connect equal parts. Words are paired with words, phrases with phrases, clauses with clauses, and sentences with sentences. All these pairs must be *parallel;* they must have the same form.

NO: Her family went to London, to Amsterdam, and they even saw Rome and Paris!

YES: Her family went to London, to Amsterdam, and even to Rome and Paris!

NO: You can use this form to apply or if you want to change your status.

YES: You can use this form to apply or to change your status.

NO: Debby noticed the way Margie talked and how she kept looking at the desk.

YES: Debby noticed how Margie talked and how she kept looking at the desk.

Pairs of connectives, such as *both/and, either/or, neither/nor,* and *not only/but also,* usually connect parallel structures.

NO: That book was both helpful and contained a lot of information.

YES: That book was both helpful and informative.

NO: So, my father said, "Either you come with us now, or stay here alone."

YES: So, my father said, "Either you come with us now, or you stay here alone."

NO: Here we either turn left or right, but I forget which.

YES: Here we turn either left or right, but I forget which.

NO: Karen bought the table both for beauty and utility.

YES: Karen bought the table for both beauty and utility.

11.4 Sentence Fragments

"Where did you go?"

"To the new movie theater. The one on Valley Street."

"Where on Valley Street?"

"Just past the train station, and across the street from the post office."

"See a good movie?"

"The best. Really funny, but serious, too."

"Sounds good."

Probably neither of the people in the conversation above realized that they were not using complete sentences. Only the first question, *"Where did you go?"* is a complete sentence. The rest are *sentence fragments.*

A sentence fragment is only a part of a sentence, because it is usually missing a subject or a verb.

NO: So illogical!

YES: It is so illogical!

NO:	Only for love, you see.
YES:	They did it only for love, you see.
NO:	No one. Not even the teacher.
YES:	No one, not even the teacher, could do it.

In conversation (as in the one above), there is a tendency to speak in sentence fragments, and so such fragments often appear in our writing. Proofreading and revision, however, can help to correct this error.

There are two ways to correct a sentence fragment. The first is to supply whatever is missing, as was done above. The other way is to attach the fragment to the sentence before or after it.

NO:	When I jog, especially in the early morning. I sometimes see the morning star.
YES:	When I jog, especially in the early morning, I sometimes see the morning star.
NO:	Because he was wrong. That's why he was embarrassed.
YES:	He was embarrassed because he was wrong.
NO:	Always and everywhere. She thought of him always and everywhere.
YES:	Always and everywhere, she thought of him.

It is not always incorrect to use sentence fragments. They are used to reproduce conversation and are also quite effective as questions and exclamations. Some examples are

How absurd!

Now for some examples.

After all this? Not on your life!

The more we studied, the less we knew.

Although properly used sentence fragments can add spark, it is generally best to avoid using them except when more liveliness is needed.

11.5 Run-On Sentences

A *run-on sentence* contains two complete sentences totally fused.

NO: It was a pleasant drive the sun was shining.

YES: It was a pleasant drive because the sun was shining.

NO: They are all similar materials they may not look or feel alike.

YES: They are all similar materials, although they may not look or feel alike.

NO: Susan said we passed the restaurant I think it's farther ahead.

YES: Susan said we passed the restaurant. I think it's farther ahead.

11.6 Comma Splices

The run-on sentence is a very common error. Sometimes a writer will try to correct it by inserting a comma between the clauses, but this creates another error, a *comma splice*. The following examples illustrate various ways to correct the comma splice.

NO: Talk softly, someone is listening.

YES: Talk softly; someone is listening.

OR

Talk softly, because someone is listening.

NO: If you know, you must tell us, we will do it.

YES: If you know, you must tell us. Then we will do it.

NO: Take a hint from me, drive more slowly on this curve.

YES: Take a hint from me: drive more slowly on this curve.

NO: We were lost, the captain could not see the land.

YES: We were lost. The captain could not see the land.

11.7 Short, Choppy Sentences—Sentence Variation

Try to read the following passage:

There was a table set out under a tree. It was in front of the house. The March Hare and the Hatter were having tea at it. A Dormouse was sitting between them. He was fast asleep. The other two were using it as a cushion. They rested their elbows on it. They talked over its head. "Very uncomfortable for the Dormouse," thought Alice; "only, as it's asleep, I suppose it doesn't mind."

Notice how quickly you read when the sentences are short; you hardly have enough time to form a picture of the scene. It is as if the writer added each thought as it occurred to him, and in fact, this is usually the case. It is a sure sign of poor writing. Now read the same excerpt the way that Lewis Carroll wrote it.

There was a table set out under a tree in front of the house, and the March Hare and the Hatter were having tea at it: a Dormouse was sitting between them, fast asleep, and the other two were using it as a cushion, resting their elbows on it and talking over its head. "Very uncomfortable for the Dormouse," thought Alice; "only, as it's asleep, I suppose it doesn't mind."

Sentence variation creates well-balanced, smooth writing that flows and gives the reader the feeling that the writer knows the subject. Although there is nothing grammatically wrong with short sentences, they often separate ideas that should be brought together.

NO: People change. Places change. Alan felt this. He had been away for ten years.

YES: On returning after a ten-year absence, Alan had a strong feeling of how people and places change.

NO: She looked at the sky. Then she looked at the sea. They were too big. She threw a rock in the ocean. She started to cry. Then she went home.

YES: The sky and the sea looked too big. She threw a rock into the ocean, and as it disappeared she began to cry. Then she turned to go home.

As a rule, avoid using chains of short, choppy sentences. Organize your thoughts and try to vary the length of your sentences.

11.8 Wordiness

Effective writing means concise writing. *Wordiness,* on the other hand, decreases clarity of expression by cluttering sentences with unnecessary words. Of course, short sentences are not necessarily better than long ones simply because they are brief. As long as a word serves a function, it should remain in the sentence. However, repetition of words, sounds, and phrases should be used only for emphasis or other stylistic reasons. Editing your writing will reduce its bulk. Notice the difference in impact between the first and second sentences in the following pairs.

NO: The medical exam that he gave me was entirely complete.

YES: The medical exam he gave me was complete.

NO: It seems perfectly clear to me that although he went and got permission from the professor, he still should not have played that awful, terrible joke on the dean.

YES: It seems clear to me that although he got permission from the professor, he still should not have played that terrible joke on the dean.

NO: It will be our aim to ensure proper health care for each and every one of the people in the United States.

YES: Our aim will be to ensure proper health care for all Americans.

11.9 Rambling Sentences

A rambling sentence continues on and on and seems to never end.

NO: The mountain was steep, but the road was clear; the sun was shining, and we all had the spirit of adventure in our heart and a song of the open road on our lips, so we took the turn that took our car up that steep mountain road.

YES: The mountain was steep, but the road was clear. The sun was shining. All of us had the spirit of adventure in our heart and a song of the open road on our lips. So we took our car up that steep mountain road.

There is often nothing grammatically wrong with a rambling sentence; it is simply too long, and it interferes with the reader's comprehension. Unfortunately, a writer who makes this kind of error tends to do it a lot. A good rule to follow is this: If a sentence runs for more than two typewritten lines, think twice about it. It should probably be recast.

CHAPTER 12

Glossary of Usage

The complex nature of language sometimes makes writing difficult. Words often become confusing when they have similar forms and sounds. Indeed, an author may have a correct meaning in mind, but an incorrect word choice can alter the meaning of a sentence or even make it totally illogical.

NO: Martha was always part of that *cliché*.

YES: Martha was always part of that *clique*.
      (A *cliché* is a trite or hackneyed expression; a *clique* is an exclusive group of people.)

NO: The minister spoke of the soul's *immorality*.

YES: The minister spoke of the soul's *immortality*.
      (*Immorality* means wickedness; *immortality* means imperishable or unending life.)

NO: Where is the nearest *stationary* store?

YES: Where is the nearest *stationery* store?
      (*Stationary* means immovable; *stationery* is paper used for writing.)

12.1   Words Commonly Confused and Misused

Below are groups of words that are often confused because of their similar forms and sounds.

1. *a*   *A* is used before words beginning with a consonant sound.

   an   *An* is used before words with a vowel sound. This is an important distinction; it is not the spelling that determines whether to use *a* or *an,* but the sound.

an umbrella	BUT a university
a radio	BUT an RCA record
an hour	BUT a human being
a historical event	BUT an honorary degree

2. accent   v. to stress or emphasize. (You must *accent* the last syllable.)

   ascent   n. a climb or rise. (John's *ascent* of the mountain was dangerous.)

   assent   n. consent, compliance. (We need your *assent* before we can go ahead with the plans.)

3. accept   v. to take something offered. (She *accepted* the gift.)

   except   prep. other than, but. (Everyone was included in the plans *except* him.)

4. advice   n. opinion given as to what to do or how to handle a situation. (Her sister gave her *advice* on what to say at the interview.)

   advise   v. to counsel. (John's guidance counselor *advised* him on which colleges to apply to.)

5. affect   v. to influence. (Mary's suggestion did not *affect* me.)

   effect   v. to cause to happen. (The plan was *effected* with great success.)   n. result. (The *effect* of the medicine is excellent.)

6. allusion   n. indirect reference. (In the poem, there are many biblical *allusions.*)

	illusion	n. false idea or conception; belief or opinion not in accord with the facts. (Greg was under the *illusion* that he could win the race after missing three weeks of practice.)
7.	already	adv. previously. (I had *already* read that novel.)
	all ready	adv. + adj. prepared. (The family was *all ready* to leave on vacation.)
8.	altar	n. table or stand used in religious rites. (The priest stood at the *altar.*)
	alter	v. to change. (Their plans were *altered* during the strike.)
9.	as if	conj. as it would be if (It looks *as if* it's going to rain.)
	like	prep. inclined to (It looks *like* rain.)
10.	capital	n. 1. a city where the government meets. (The senators had a meeting in Albany, the *capital* of New York.) 2. money used in business. (They had enough *capital* to develop the industry.)
	capitol	n. building in which the legislature meets. (Senator Brown gave a speech at the *Capitol* in Washington.)
11.	choose	v. to select. (Which camera did you *choose*?)
	chose	past tense, choose. (Susan *chose* to stay home.)
12.	cite	v. to quote. (The student *cited* evidence from the text.)
	site	n. location. (They chose the *site* where the house would be built.)
13.	clothes	n. garments. (Because she got caught in the rain, her *clothes* were wet.)
	cloths	n. pieces of material. (The *cloths* were used to wash the windows.)

14. coarse   adj. rough, unrefined. (Sandpaper is *coarse*.)

     course   n. 1. path of action. (She did not know what *course* would solve the problem.)
2. passage. (We took the long *course* to the lake.)
3. series of studies. (We both enrolled in the physics *course*.) 4. part of a meal. (She served a five-*course* meal.)

15. consul   n. a person appointed by the government to live in a foreign city and represent the citizenry and business interests of the native country there. (The *consul* was appointed to Naples, Italy.)

     council   n. a group used for discussion or advisement. (The *council* decided to accept his letter of resignation.)

     counsel   v. to advise. (Tom *counsels* Jerry on tax matters.)

16. criterion   n. (singular) standard (The only *criterion* is patience.)

     criteria   (plural) (There are several *criteria* applicants must meet.)

17. decent   adj. proper; respectable. (He was very *decent* about the entire matter.)

     descent   n. 1. moving down. (In Dante's *Inferno*, the *descent* into hell was depicted graphically.) 2. ancestry. (He is of Irish *descent*.)

18. device   n. 1. plan; scheme. (The *device* helped her win the race.) 2. invention. (We bought a *device* that opens the garage door automatically.)

     devise   v. to contrive. (He *devised* a plan so John could not win.)

19. emigrate   v. to go away from a country. (Many Japanese *emigrated* from Japan in the late 1800s.)

     immigrate   v. to come into a country. (Her relatives *immigrated* to the United States after World War I.)

20.	eminent	n. prominent. (He is an *eminent* member of the community.)
	imminent	adj. impending. (The decision is *imminent*.)
	immanent	adj. existing within. (Maggie believed that religious spirit is *immanent* in human beings.)
21.	fair	adj. 1. beautiful. (She was a *fair* maiden.) 2. just. (She tried to be *fair*.) n. festival. (There were many games at the *fair*.)
	fare	n. amount of money paid for transportation. (The city proposed that the subway *fare* be raised.)
22.	farther	adv. distance. (We travelled farther than we expected.)
	further	adv. furthermore; in depth. (We will discuss this *further*.)
23.	forth	adv. onward. (The soldiers moved *forth* in the blinding snow.)
	fourth	adj. 4th. (She was the *fourth* runner-up in the beauty contest.)
24.	imply	v. to suggest something. (I *implied* that I didn't approve of their actions.)
	infer	v. to drawer a conclusion from a remark or action. (I *inferred* from your letter that you will not be attending the meeting next week.)
25.	insure	v. to guarantee. (He *insured* his luggage before the flight.)
	ensure	v. to make certain. (*Ensure* your safety by driving carefully.)
26.	its	possessive form of *it*. (Our town must improve *its* roads.)
	it's	contraction of *it is*. (*It's* time to leave the party.)
27.	later	adj., adv. at a subsequent date. (We will take a vacation *later* this year.)

	latter	n. second of the two. (Susan can visit Monday or Tuesday. The *latter,* however, is preferable.)
28.	lead	n. a metal. (The handgun was made of *lead.*) v. to show the way. (The camp counselor *leads* the way to the picnic grounds.)
	led	past tense of verb *lead.* (The dog *led* the way.)
29.	lend	v. to let out for temporary use. (We are in the business of *lending* you money.)
	loan	n. money lent at interest. (The bank gave the student a *loan* for her tuition.)
30.	loose	adj. free, unrestricted. (The dog was let *loose* by accident.)
	lose	v. to suffer the loss of. (He was afraid he would *lose* the race.)
31.	moral	adj. virtuous. (She is a *moral* woman with high ethical standards.) n. lesson taught by a story, incident, etc. (Most fables end with a *moral.*)
	morale	n. mental condition. (After the team lost the game, their *morale* was low.)
32.	of	prep. from. (She is *of* French descent.)
	off	adv. away, at a distance. (The television fell *off* the table.)
33.	passed	past tense of verb *pass.* having satisfied some requirement. (He *passed* the test.)
	past	adj. gone by or elapsed in time. (His *past* deeds got him in trouble.) n. a period of time gone by. (His *past* was shady.) prep. beyond. (She ran *past* the house.)
34.	personal	adj. private. (Jack was unwilling to discuss his childhood; it was too *personal.*)
	personnel	n. staff. (The *personnel* at the department store was made up of young adults.)

35.	principal	n. head of a school. (The *principal* addressed the graduating class.) adj. main, most important. (JR was the *principal* character in the TV drama "Dallas.") or (The country's *principal* export is coffee.)
	principle	n. the ultimate source, origin, or cause of something; a law, truth. (The *principles* of physics were reviewed in class today.)
36.	prophecy	n. prediction of the future. (His *prophecy* that he would become a doctor came true.)
	prophesy	v. to declare or predict. (He *prophesied* that we would win the lottery.)
37.	quiet	adj. still; calm. (At night, all is *quiet*.)
	quite	adv. really, truly. (She is *quite* a good singer.)
	quit	v. to free oneself. (Peter had little time to spare, so he *quit* the chorus.)
38.	respectfully	adv. with respect, honor, esteem. (He declined the offer *respectfully*.)
	respectively	adv. in the order mentioned. (Jack, Susan, and Jim, who are members of the club, were elected president, vice president, and secretary, *respectively*.)
39.	stationary	adj. immovable. (The park bench is *stationary*.)
	stationery	n. paper used for writing. (The invitations were printed on yellow *stationery*.)
40.	straight	adj. not curved. (The road was *straight*.)
	strait	adj. restricted, narrow, confined. (The patient was put into a *strait* jacket.) n. narrow waterway. (He sailed through the *Straits* of Magellan.)
41.	than	conj. used most commonly in comparisons. (Maggie is older *than* I.)
	then	adv. soon afterward. (We lived in Boston; *then* we moved to New York.)

42.	their	possessive form of *they*. (That is *their* house on Tenafly Drive.)
	they're	contraction of *they are*. (*They're* leaving for California next week.)
	there	adv. at that place. (Who is standing *there* under the tree?)
43.	to	prep. in the direction of; toward. (She made a turn *to* the right onto Norman Street.)
	too	adv. 1. more than enough. (She served *too* much for dinner.) 2. also. (He is going to Maine *too*.)
	two	n. 2; the sum of one plus one. (We have *two* pet rabbits.)
44.	weather	n. the general condition of the atmosphere. (The *weather* is expected to be clear on Sunday.)
	whether	conj. if it be a case or fact. (We don't know *whether* the trains are late.)
45.	who's	contraction of *who is* or *who has*. (*Who's* willing to volunteer for the night shift?)
	whose	possessive form of *who*. (*Whose* book is this?)
46.	your	possessive form of *you*. (Is this *your* seat?)
	you're	contraction of *you are*. (I know *you're* going to do well on the test.)

CHAPTER 13

End Punctuation Marks

Try to read this paragraph.

take some more tea the march hare said to alice very earnestly ive had nothing yet alice replied in an offended tone so i cant take more you mean you cant take less said the hatter its very easy to take more than nothing lewis carroll

Now try again.

"Take some more tea," the March Hare said to Alice, very earnestly.

"I've had nothing yet," Alice replied in an offended tone, "so I can't take more."

"You mean you can't take less," said the Hatter. "It's very easy to take more than nothing."

—Lewis Carroll

This example illustrates to what extent punctuation helps the reader understand what the writer is trying to say. The most important role of punctuation is clarification.

In speech, words are accompanied by gesture, voice, tone, and rhythm that help convey a desired meaning. In writing, it is punctuation alone that must do the same job.

There are many rules about how to use the various punctuation marks. These are sometimes difficult to understand, because they are described with so much grammatical terminology. Therefore, this discussion of punctuation will avoid as much terminology as possible. If you still find the rules confusing, and your method of punctuation is somewhat random, try to remember that most punctuation takes the place of pauses in speech.

Keeping this in mind, read your sentences aloud as you write; if you punctuate according to the pauses in your voice, you will do much better than if you put in your commas, periods, and dashes either at random or where they look good.

There are three ways to end a sentence.

1. a period

2. a question mark

3. an exclamation point

13.1 The Period

Periods end all sentences that are not questions or exclamations. In speech, the end of a sentence is indicated with a full pause. The period is the written counterpart of this pause.

Go get me my paper. I'm anxious to see the news.

Into each life some rain must fall. Last night some fell into mine.

When a question is intended as a suggestion and the listener is not expected to answer or when a question is asked indirectly as part of a sentence, a period is also used.

Mimi wondered if the parade would ever end.

Will you please send the flowers you advertised.

We'll never know who the culprit was.

Periods also follow most abbreviations and contractions.

Wed.	Dr.	Jr.	Sr.
etc.	Jan.	Mr.	Mr.
Esq.	cont.	a.m.	A.D.

Periods (or parentheses) are also used after a letter or number in a series.

a. apples	1. president
b. oranges	2. vice president
c. pears	3. secretary

Errors to Avoid

Be sure to omit the period after a quotation mark preceded by a period. Only one stop is necessary to end a sentence.

She said, "Hold my hand." (no period after the final quotation mark)

"Don't go into the park until later."

"It's not my fault," he said. "She would have taken the car anyway."

After many abbreviations, particularly those of organizations or agencies, no period is used (check in a dictionary if in doubt).

AFL-CIO	NAACP	GM
FBI	NATO	IBM
TV	UN	HEW

13.2 The Question Mark

Use a *question mark* to end a direct question even if it is not in the form of a question. The question mark in writing denotes the rising tone of voice used to indicate a question in speech. If you read the following two sentences aloud, you will see the difference in tone between a statement and a question composed of the same words.

Mary is here.

Mary is here?

Here are some more examples of correct use of the question mark. Pay special attention to the way it is used with other punctuation.

Where will we go next?

"Won't you," he asked, "please lend me a hand?"

"Will they ever give us our freedom?" the prisoner asked.

Who asked, "When?"

Question marks indicate a full stop and lend a different emphasis to a sentence than do commas. Compare these pairs of sentences.

Was the sonata by Beethoven? or Brahms? or Chopin?

Was the sonata by Beethoven, or Brahms, or Chopin?

Did they walk to the park? climb the small hill? take the bus to town? or go skating out back?

Did they walk to town, climb the small hill, take the bus to town, or go skating out back?

Sometimes question marks are placed in parentheses. This indicates doubt or uncertainty about the facts being reported.

The bombing started at 3 a.m.(?)

She said the dress cost $200,000.(?)

Harriet Stacher (18(?)-1914) was well thought of in her time.

Hippocrates (460(?)-(?)377 B.C.) is said to be the father of modern medicine.

13.3   The Exclamation Point

An *exclamation point* ends an emphatic statement. It should be used only to express strong emotions, such as surprise, disbelief, or admiration. If it is used too often for mild expressions of emotion, it loses its effectiveness.

Let go of me!

Help! Fire!

It was a wonderful day!

What a beautiful woman she is!

Who shouted "Fire!" *(Notice no question mark is necessary)*

Fantastic!

"Unbelievable!" she gasped. *(Notice no comma is necessary)*

"You'll never win!" he cried.

Where else can I go! *(The use of the exc!amation point shows that this is a strong statement even though it is worded like a question.)*

Do not overuse exclamation points. The following is an example of the overuse of exclamation points:

Dear Susan,

I was so glad to see you last week! You looked better than ever! Our talk meant so much to me! I can hardly wait until we get together again! Could you believe how long it has been! Let's never let that happen again! Please write as soon as you get the chance! I can hardly wait to hear from you!

Your friend,

Nora

13.3.1 Interjections

An *interjection* is a word or group of words used as an exclamation to express emotion. It need not be followed by an exclamation point. Often an interjection is followed by a comma (see **The Comma**) if it is not very intense. Technically, the interjection has no grammatical relation to other words in the sentence; yet it is still considered a part of speech.

Oh dear, I forgot my keys again.

Ah! Now do you understand?

Ouch! I didn't realize that the stove was hot.

Oh, excuse me. I didn't realize that you were next on line.

CHAPTER 14

Internal Punctuation Marks

14.1 The Comma

Of all the marks of punctuation, the comma (,) has the most uses. Before you tackle the main principles that guide its usage, be sure that you have an elementary understanding of sentence structure. There are actually only a few rules and conventions to follow when using commas; the rest is common sense. The worst abuse of commas comes from those who overuse them or who place them illogically. If you are ever in doubt as to whether or not to use a comma, do not use it.

14.1.1 In A Series

When more than one adjective (an adjective series) describes a noun, use a comma to separate and emphasize each adjective.

the long, dark passageway

another confusing, sleepless night

an elaborate, complex plan

In these instances, the comma takes the place of "and." To test if the comma is needed, try inserting "and" between the adjectives in question. If it is logical, you should use a comma. The following are examples of adjectives that describe an adjective-noun combination that has come to be thought of almost as one word. In such cases, the adjective in front of the adjective-noun combination needs no comma.

99

a stately *oak tree*	my worst *report card*
an exceptional *wine glass*	a borrowed *record player*
a successful *garage sale*	a porcelain *dinner plate*

If you insert "and" between the adjectives in the above examples, it will not make sense.

The comma is also used to separate words, phrases, and whole ideas (clauses); it still takes the place of "and" when used this way.

an apple, a pear, a fig, and a banana

a lovely lady, an indecent dress, and many admirers

She lowered the shade, closed the curtain, turned off the light, and went to bed.

John, Frank, and my Uncle Harry all thought it was a questionable theory.

The only question that exists about the use of commas in a series is whether or not one should be used before the final item. Usually "and" or "or" precedes the final item, and many writers do not include the comma before the final "and" or "or." However, it is advisable to use the comma, because often its omission can be confusing—in such cases as these, for instance.

NO: Would you like to shop at Saks, Lord and Taylor and Macy's?

NO: He got on his horse, tracked a rabbit and a deer and rode on to Canton.

NO: We planned the trip with Mary and Harold, Susan, Dick and Joan, Gregory and Jean and Charles. *(Is it Gregory and Jean or Jean and Charles or Gregory and Jean and Charles?)*

14.1.2 With Introductory Words, Phrases, and Clauses

Usually if a phrase or clause precedes the subject at the beginning of a sentence, a comma is used to set it off.

After last night's fiasco at the disco, she couldn't bear the thought of looking at him again. (introductory phrase)

Whenever I try to talk about politics, my husband leaves the room. (introductory clause)

If an introductory phrase includes a verb form that is being used as another part of speech (a "verbal"), it must be followed by a comma. Introductory elliptical clauses must also be followed by a comma. Try to make sense of the following sentences without commas.

NO: When eating Mary never looked up from her plate.

YES: When eating, Mary never looked up from her plate. (elliptical clause)

NO: Because of her desire to follow her faith in James wavered.

YES: Because of her desire to follow, her faith in James wavered.

Above all, common sense is the best guideline when trying to decide whether or not to use a comma after an introductory phrase. Does the comma make the meaning clearer? If it does, use it; if not, there is no reason to insert it.

14.1.3 To Separate Sentences with Two Main Ideas (Compound Sentences)

To understand this use of the comma, you need to have studied sentence structure and be able to recognize compound sentences.

When a sentence contains more than two subjects and verbs (clauses) and the two clauses are joined by a connecting word (*and, but, or, yet, for, nor*), use a comma before the connecting word to show that another clause is coming.

I thought I knew the poem by heart, but he showed me three lines I had forgotten.

Are we really interested in helping the children, or are we more concerned with protecting our good names?

If the two parts of the sentence are short and closely related, it is not necessary to use a comma.

He threw the ball and the dog ran after it.

Jane played the piano and Charles danced.

Errors to Avoid

Be careful not to confuse a compound sentence with a sentence that has a compound verb and a single subject. If the subject is the same for both verbs, there is no need for a comma.

> NO: Charles sent some flowers, and wrote a long letter explaining why he had not been able to come.

> NO: Last Thursday we went to the concert with Julia, and afterward dined at an old Italian restaurant.

14.1.4 With Interrupting Material

There are so many different kinds of interruptions that can occur in a sentence that a list of them all would be quite lengthy. In general, words and phrases that stop the flow of the sentence or are unnecessary for the main idea are set off by commas.

Abbreviations after names

Did you invite John Paul, Jr., and his sister?

Interjections: An exclamation added without grammatical connection.

Oh, I'm so glad to see you.

Direct address

Roy, won't you open the door for the dog?

I can't understand, Mother, what you are trying to say.

Tag questions: A question that repeats the helping verb and is in the negative.

I'm really hungry, aren't you?

Jerry looks like his father, doesn't he?

Geographical names and addresses

The concert will be held in Chicago, Illinois, on August 12.

The letter was addressed to Ms. Marion Heartwell, 1881 Pine Lane, Palo Alto, California 95824. *(No comma is used before a zip code.)*

Transitional words and phrases

On the other hand, I hope he gets better.

You'll find, therefore, no one more loyal to you than I.

Parenthetical words and phrases

You will become, I believe, a great statesman.

We know, of course, that this is the only thing to do.

Unusual word order

The dress, new and crisp, hung in the closet. *(Normal word order: The new, crisp dress hung in the closet.)*

Intently, she stared out the window. *(Normal word order: She stared intently out the window.)*

14.1.5 With Nonrestrictive Elements (Not Essential to the Meaning)

Parts of a sentence that modify other parts are sometimes essential to the meaning of the sentence and sometimes not. When a modifying word or group of words is not vital to the meaning of the sentence, it is set off by commas. Since it does not restrict the meaning of the words it modifies, it is called "nonrestrictive." Modifiers that are essential to the meaning of the sentence are called "restrictive" and are not set off by commas. Compare the following pairs of sentences:

The girl *who wrote the story* is my sister. (essential)

My sister, *the girl who wrote the story,* has always been drawn to adventure. (nonessential)

The cup *that is on the piano* is the one I want. (essential)

The cup, *which my brother gave me last year,* is on the piano. (nonessential)

She always listened to her sister *Jean.* (essential—she must have more than one sister)

She always listened to her husband, *Jack.* (nonessential—obviously, she has only one husband)

14.1.6   With Direct Quotations

Most direct quotes or quoted materials are set off from the rest of the sentence by commas.

"Please read your part more loudly," the director insisted.

"I won't know what to do," said Michael, "if you leave me now."

Mark looked up from his work, smiled, and said, "We'll be with you in a moment."

Be careful not to set off indirect quotations or quotes that are used as subjects or complements.

"To be or not to be" is the famous beginning of a soliloquy in Shakespeare's *Hamlet.* (subject)

Back then my favorite song was "A Summer Place." (complement)

She said she would never come back. (indirect quote)

14.1.7   With Contrasting Elements

Her intelligence, *not her beauty,* got her the job.

Your plan will take you further from, *rather than closer to,* your destination.

14.1.8   With Dates

Both forms of the date are acceptable.

She will arrive on April 6, 1995.

He left on 5 December 1994.

In January 1995 he handed in his resignation.

In January, 1995, he handed in his resignation.

14.2 The Semicolon

Semicolons (;) are sometimes called mild periods. They indicate a pause midway in length between the comma and the colon. Writing that contains many semicolons is usually in a dignified, formal style. To use them correctly, it is necessary to be able to recognize main clauses—complete ideas. When two main clauses occur in a single sentence without a connecting word *(and, but, or, nor, for)*, the appropriate mark of punctuation is the semicolon.

It is not a good idea for you to leave the country right now; you should actually try to stay as long as you possibly can.

In the past, boy babies were often dressed in blue; girls, in pink. *("Were often dressed" is understood in the second part of the sentence.)*

Burgundy and maroon are very similar colors; scarlet is altogether different.

Notice how the use of the comma, period, and semicolon gives a sentence a slightly different meaning.

Music lightens life; literature deepens it.

Just as music lightens life, literature deepens it.

Music lightens life. Literature deepens it.

The semicolon lends a certain balance to writing that would otherwise be difficult to achieve. Nonetheless, you should be careful not to overuse it. A comma can just as well join parts of a sentence with two main ideas; the semicolon is particularly appropriate if there is a striking contrast in the two ideas expressed.

Ask not what your country can do for you; ask what you can do for your country.

It started out as an ordinary day; it ended being the most extraordinary of her life.

If any one of the following words or phrases is used to join together compound sentences, it is generally preceded by a semicolon.

then	however	thus	furthermore
hence	indeed	consequently	also

that is	nevertheless	anyhow	in addition
in fact	on the other hand	likewise	moreover
still	meanwhile	instead	besides
otherwise	in other words	henceforth	for example
therefore	at the same time	even now	nonetheless

For a long time, people thought that women were inferior to men; *even now* it is not an easy attitude to overcome.

Being clever and cynical, he succeeded in becoming president of the company; *meanwhile,* his wife left him.

Cigarette smoking has never interested me; *furthermore,* I couldn't care less if anyone else smokes or not.

When a series of complicated items is listed or if there is internal punctuation in a series, the semicolon is sometimes used to make the meaning clearer.

You can use your new car for many things: to drive to town or to the country; to impress your friends and neighbors; to protect yourself from rain on a trip away from home; and to borrow against should you need money right away.

The scores from yesterday's games came in late last night: Pirates-6, Zoomers-3; Caterpillars-12, Steelys-8; Crashers-9, Links-8; and Greens-15, Uptowns-4.

The semicolon is placed outside quotation marks or parentheses, unless it is a part of the material enclosed in those marks.

I used to call him "my lord and master"; it made him laugh every time.

The weather was cold for that time of year (I was shivering wherever I went); nevertheless, we set out to hike to the top of that mountain.

14.3 The Colon

The *colon* (:) is the sign of a pause about midway in length between the semicolon and the period. It can often be replaced by a comma and sometimes by a period. Although used less frequently now than it was 50 to 75 years ago, the colon is still convenient to use, for it signals to the reader that more information is to come on the subject of concern. The colon can also create a slight dramatic tension.

It is used to introduce a word, a phrase, or a complete statement (clause) that emphasizes, illustrates, or exemplifies what has already been stated.

He had only one desire in life: to play baseball.

The weather that day was the most unusual I'd ever seen: it snowed and rained while the sun was still shining.

Since the colon is not an end mark (used to end a sentence), do not capitalize after the colon unless the word is a proper noun.

May I offer you a suggestion: don't drive without your seat belts fastened.

The thought continued to perplex him: where will I go next?

When introducing a series that illustrates or emphasizes what has already been stated, use the colon.

Only a few of the graduates were able to be there: Jamison, Mearns, Linkley, and Commoner.

For Omar Khayyam, a Persian poet, three things are necessary for a paradise on earth: a loaf of bread, a jug of wine, and one's beloved.

Long quotations set off from the rest of the text by indentation rather than quotation marks are generally introduced with a colon.

The first line of Lincoln's Gettysburg address is familiar to most Americans:

Four score and seven years ago our fathers brought forth on this continent a new nation, conceived in liberty and dedicated to the proposition that all men are created equal.

I quote from Shakespeare's *Sonnets*:

When I do count the clock that tells the time,
And see the brave day sunk in hideous night;
When I behold the violet past prime,

And sable curls all silver'd o'er with white…

It is also customary to begin a business letter with a colon.

Dear Senator Jordan:

To Whom It May Concern:

Gentlemen:

Dear Sir or Madam:

In informal letters, use a comma.

Dear Mary,

Dear Father,

The colon is also used in introducing a list.

Please send the following:

1. 50 index cards

2. 4 typewriter ribbons

3. 8 erasers

Prepare the recipe as follows:

1. Slice the oranges thinly.

2. Arrange them in a circle around the strawberries.

3. Pour the liqueur over both fruits.

At least three ladies will have to be there to help:

1. Mrs. Goldman, who will greet the guests;

2. Harriet Sacher, who will serve the lunch; and

3. my sister, who will do whatever else needs to be done.

Finally, the colon is used between numbers when writing the time, between the volume and number or volume and page number of a journal, and between the chapter and verse in the Bible.

4:30 P.M.

The Nation, 34:8

Genesis 5:18

14.4 The Dash

Use the *dash* (—) to indicate a sudden or unexpected break in the normal flow of the sentence. It can also be used in place of parentheses or of commas if the meaning is clarified. Usually the dash gives special emphasis to the material it sets off. On a typewriter, two hyphens (--) indicate a dash.

Could you—I hate to ask!—help me with these boxes?

When we left town—a day never to be forgotten—they had a record snowfall.

She said—we all heard it—"The safe is not locked."

A dash is often used to summarize a series of ideas that have already been expressed.

Freedom of speech, freedom to vote, and freedom of assembly—these are the cornerstones of democracy.

Carbohydrates, fats, and proteins—these are the basic kinds of food we need.

The dash is also used to note the author of a quotation that is set off in the text.

Nothing is good or bad but thinking makes it so.

—William Shakespeare

14.5 Parentheses

To set off material that is only loosely connected to the central meaning of the sentence, use *parentheses* [( )].

Most men (at least, most that I know) like wine, women, and song but have too much work and not enough time for such enjoyments.

On Tuesday evenings and Thursday afternoons (the times I don't have classes), the television programs are not too exciting.

Watch out for other punctuation when you use parentheses. Punctuation that refers to the material enclosed in the parentheses occurs inside the marks. Punctuation belonging to the rest of the sentence comes outside the parentheses.

I thought I knew the poem by heart (boy, was I wrong!).

For a long time (too long as far as I'm concerned), women were thought to be inferior to men.

We must always strive to tell the truth. (Are we even sure we know what truth is?)

When I first saw a rose (don't you think it's the most beautiful flower?), I thought it must be man-made.

14.6 Quotation Marks

The proper use of quotation marks must be studied and learned, because some of their uses appear arbitrary and outside common sense.

The most common use of double quotation marks (" ") is to set off quoted words, phrases, and sentences.

"If everybody minded their own business," said the duchess in a hoarse growl, "the world would go round a great deal faster than it does."

"Then you would say what you mean," the March Hare went on.

"I do," Alice hastily replied: "At least—at least I mean what I say—that's the same thing, you know."

"Not the same thing a bit!" said the Hatter. "Why, you might just as well say that 'I see what I eat' is the same thing as 'I eat what I see'!"

Both quotes from Lewis Carroll's
Alice in Wonderland

In the latter quote, single quotation marks are used to set off quoted material within a quote. Other examples of correct use of single quotation marks:

"Shall I bring 'Rime of the Ancient Mariner' along with us?" she asked her brother.

Mrs. Green said, "The doctor told me, 'Go immediately to bed when you get home.'"

14.6.1 With Commas and Periods

Remember that commas and periods are always placed inside quotation marks even if they are not actually part of the quote.

NO: "Get down here right away", John cried. "You'll miss the sunset if you don't".

YES: "Get down here right away," John cried. "You'll miss the sunset if you don't."

NO: "If my dog could talk", Mary mused, "I'll bet he would say 'Take me for a walk right this minute.'"

YES: "If my dog could talk," Mary mused, "I'll bet he would say 'Take me for a walk right this minute.'"

14.6.2 With Question Marks and Exclamation Points

Other marks of punctuation, such as question marks, exclamation points, colons, and semicolons, go inside the quotation marks if they are part of the quoted material. If they are not part of the quote, however, they go outside the quotation marks. Be careful to distinguish between the guidelines for the comma and period, which *always* go inside the quotation marks, and those for the other marks of punctuation.

NO: Did you hear her say, "He'll be there early?" *(The question mark belongs to the entire sentence and not to the quote alone.)*

YES: Did you hear her say, "He'll be there early"?

NO: She called down the stairs, "When are you coming"? *(The question mark belongs to the quote.)*

YES: She called down the stairs, "When are you coming?"

NO: "Ask not what your country can do for you"; said Kennedy, "ask what you can do for your country:" a statement of genius I think. *(The semicolon is part of the quoted material; the colon is not part of the quote but belongs to the entire sentence.)*

111

YES: "Ask not what your country can do for you;" said Kennedy, "ask what you can do for your country": a statement of genius, I think.

NO: "Let me out"! he cried. "Don't you have any pity"?

YES: "Let me out!" he cried. "Don't you have any pity?"

Remember to use only one mark of punctuation at the end of a sentence ending with a quotation.

NO: She thought aloud, "Will I ever finish this paper in time for that class?".

YES: She thought aloud, "Will I ever finish this paper in time for that class?"

NO: "Not the same thing a bit!", said the Hatter. "Why, you might just as well say that 'I see what I eat' is the same thing as 'I eat what I see'!".

YES: "Not the same thing a bit!" said the Hatter. "Why, you might just as well say that 'I see what I eat' is the same thing as 'I eat what I see'!"

14.6.3 Writing Dialogue

When writing dialogue, begin a new paragraph each time the speaker changes.

"Do you know what time it is?" asked Jane. "I don't want to be late for my class."

"Can't you see I'm busy?" snapped Mary. "Go into the kitchen if you want the time."

"It's easy to see you're in a bad mood today," replied Jane.

Use quotation marks to enclose words used as words. Sometimes italics are used for this purpose.

"Judgment" had always been a difficult word for me to spell.

I always thought *"nice"* meant *"particular"* or *"having exacting standards,"* but I know now it has acquired a much more general and vague meaning.

If slang is used within more formal writing, the slang words or phrases should be set off with quotation marks.

The *"old boy"* system is responsible for most promotions in today's corporate world.

Harrison's decision to leave the conference and to *"stick his neck out"* by flying to Jamaica was applauded by the rest of the participants.

When words are meant to have an unusual or special significance to the reader, for instance irony or humor, they are sometimes placed in quotation marks. This is, however, a practice to be avoided whenever possible. The reader should be able to get the intended meaning from the context.

For years, women were not allowed to buy real estate in order to *"protect"* them from unscrupulous dealers. *(The writer is using somebody else's word; the use of the quotation marks shows he or she does not believe women needed protection.)*

The *"conversation"* resulted in one black eye and a broken arm.

To set off titles of radio and TV shows, poems, stories, and chapters in a book, use quotation marks. (Book, motion picture, newspaper, and magazine titles are underlined.)

The article "Moving South in the Southern Rain," by Jergen Smith in the *Southern News,* attracted the attention of our editor.

My favorite essay by Montaigne is "On Silence."

You will find Keats' "Ode on a Grecian Urn" in chapter 3, "The Romantic Era," in Lastly's *Selections from Great English Poets.*

Errors to Avoid

Be sure to remember that quotation marks always come in pairs. Do not make the mistake of using only one set.

NO: "You'll never convince me to move to the city, said Thurman. I consider it an insane asylum."

YES: "You'll never convince me to move to the city," said Thurman. "I consider it an insane asylum."

When a quote consists of several sentences, do not put the quotation marks at the beginning and the end of each sentence; put them at the beginning and end of the entire quotation.

NO: "It was during his student days in Bonn that Beethoven fastened upon Schiller's poem." "The heady sense of liberation in the verses must have appealed to him." "They appealed to every German."

—John Burke

YES: "It was during his student days in Bonn that Beethoven fastened upon Schiller's poem. The heady sense of liberation in the verses must have appealed to him. They appealed to every German."

—John Burke

Instead of setting off a long quote with quotation marks, you may want to indent and single space it. If you do indent, do not use quotation marks.

We are not enemies, but friends. We must not be enemies. Though passion may have strained, it must not break, our bonds of affection. The mystic chords of memory, stretching from every battlefield and patriot grave to every living heart and hearthstone all over this broad land, will yet swell the chorus of the Union when again touched, as surely they will be, by the better angels of our nature.

—Abraham Lincoln, First Inaugural Address

Be careful not to use quotation marks with indirect quotations.

NO: Mary wondered "if she would ever get over it."

YES: Mary wondered if she would ever get over it.

NO: "My exercise teacher told me," Mary said, "'that I should do these back exercises 15 minutes each day.'"

YES: "My exercise teacher told me," Mary said, "that I should do these back exercises 15 minutes each day."

When you quote several paragraphs, it is not sufficient to place quotation marks at the beginning and end of the entire quote. Place quotation marks *at the beginning of each paragraph, but at the end of only the last paragraph.* Here is an abbreviated quotation for an example.

"Here begins an odyssey through the world of classical mythology, starting with the creation of the world, proceeding to the divinities that once governed all aspects of human life.

"It is true that themes similar to the classical may be found in almost any corpus of mythology. Even technology is not immune to the influence of Greece and Rome.

"We hardly need mention the extent to which painters and sculptors have used and adapted classical mythology to illustrate the past, to reveal the human body, to express romantic or antiromantic ideals, or to symbolize any particular point of view."

14.7 The Apostrophe

14.7.1 To Indicate Omission

Use the apostophe to form contractions and to indicate that letters or figures have been omitted.

can't (cannot)	o'clock (of the clock)
I'll (I will)	it's (it is)
memories of '42 (1942)	won't (will not)
you've (you have)	they're (they are)

Notice that the apostrophe is *always* placed where a letter or letters have been omitted. Avoid such careless errors as writing wo'nt instead of won't, for example. Contractions are generally not used in formal writing. They are found primarily in speech and informal writing.

14.7.2 To Indicate the Plural Form

An apostrophe is also used to indicate the plural form of letters, figures, and words that normally don't take a plural form. In such cases it might be confusing to add only an "s."

He quickly learned his *r's* and *s's*.

Most of the *Ph.D.'s* and *M.D.'s* understand the new technology they are using for anticancer drugs.

Her *2's* always looked like her *4's*.

Marion used too many *the's* and *and's* in her last paper for English literature.

Whenever possible, try to form plurals by adding only "s" to numbers and to single or multiple letters used as words.

the ABCs	the 1940s
in threes and fours	three Rs

14.7.3 To Indicate Possession

In spoken English, the same pronunciation is used for the plural, singular possessive, and plural possessive of most nouns. It is only in context that the listener is able to tell the difference in the words used by the speaker. In written English, spelling as well as context tells readers the meaning of the noun the writer is using. The writer has only to master the placement of the apostrophe so that the meaning is clearly conveyed to the reader. These words are pronounced alike but have different meanings.

PLURAL	SINGULAR POSSESSIVE	PLURAL POSSESSIVE
neighbors	neighbor's	neighbors'
doctors	doctor's	doctors'
weeks	week's	weeks'
sopranos	soprano's	sopranos'
civilizations	civilization's	civilizations'

If you aren't sure of the apostrophe's placement, you can determine it accurately by this simple test: change the possessive phrase into "belonging to" or into an "of" phrase to discover the basic noun. You will find this a particularly useful trick for some of the more confusing possessive forms, such as those on words that end in "s" or "es."

116

Keats' poem: The poem belonging to Keats. Base noun is *Keats;* possessive is Keats' or Keats's, not Keat's or Keatsies.

The Joneses' house: The house of the Joneses (plural of Jones). Base is *Joneses;* possessive is Joneses', not Jones' or Jones'es.

Four months' pay: The pay of four months. *Months* is base; possessive is months', not month's.

The lioness' strength: The strength of the lioness. *Lioness* is base; possessive is lioness' or lioness's, not lioness'es or liones's.

It is anybody's guess: The guess of anybody. *Anybody* is the base noun; possessive is anybody's, not anybodys' or anybodies'.

14.8 Italics

Italic is a particular kind of type used by printers. It is a light, thin type that slants to the right. In writing or typing, italic is indicated by underlining. Although its usage varies a great deal, there are some general guidelines that should be followed.

Italics are used most often to indicate the title of a play, book, movie, long poem, newspaper, magazine, musical composition, work of art, ship, train, or aircraft.

She had just read Kenneth Clark's *Civilization.*

Leonardo da Vinci's most famous painting must certainly be *La Gioconda* which we know as the Mona Lisa. (Traditional titles or nicknames are not underlined.)

The *New York Times* (or New York *Times*) may be the best paper in the world. (The name of the city associated with a newspaper and considered part of the title may or may not be italicized.)

The *Enola Gay* dropped the first atomic bomb on Hiroshima.

Note: When the overall text is italicized (as in the sentence below), the word that would otherwise be italicized should be in roman (straight) type to better indicate the contrast.

The Enola Gay *dropped the first atomic bomb on Hiroshima.*

Errors to Avoid

Reserve the use of quotation marks for short parts of longer works, such as stories, poems, and chapters, and for the titles of radio and TV shows. This helps distinguish the title of a book from a chapter, the name of an article from a magazine title, and a poem from the collection in which it appears.

NO: *The Southern Predicament* that ran in the *Atlantic Monthly* in February received attention from us all.

YES: "The Southern Predicament" that ran in the *Atlantic Monthly* in February received attention from us all.

NO: Chapter 6, *The Marijuana Question,* seems to me the most controversial part of *Drugs Today* by Himmel.

YES: Chapter 6, "The Marijuana Question," seems to me the most controversial part of *Drugs Today* by Himmel.

Use italics to indicate a foreign word that has not yet become part of accepted English. Refer to your dictionary in order to be sure of the status of a particular word. Examples of familiar foreign words that are already part of our language and that *should not be italicized are*

a priori	psyche	status quo
cliché	élan	ad hoc
staccato	trattoria	andante
fait accompli	ipso facto	rendezvous
tête-à-tête	dolce vita	

Some foreign phrases and words that *should be italicized are*

The Perellis all called *"arrivederci,"* as Daniel left. (Italian for "farewell")

She'd always had a *femme de chambre.* (French for "chambermaid")

When words are referred to as words, then either quotation marks or italics can be used. (See Quotation Marks)

I'm never sure whether to use "infer" or "imply."

OR

I'm never sure whether to use *infer* or *imply.*

My "2's" and "4's" look similar.

    OR

My *2's* and *4's* look similar.

Sometimes special emphasis is put on a word or phrase by underlining, italicizing, or placing it in quotation marks. Minimize this practice whenever you can; try to indicate emphasis by word order or syntax, rather than by excessive underlining, which reflects laziness on the part of the writer.

She didn't ask John to come; she asked *me.*

It's *time* that heals our wounds.

14.9 Hyphens

14.9.1 Compound Words

There are literally hundreds of rules for the use of hyphens—especially in compound words. The following are some of the most important, more dependable rules for hyphenation of compounds.

Hyphenate two or more words used as adjectives when you want to express the idea of a unit, if they come before the word they modify. If, however, they follow the main word, they should generally not be hyphenated. (See **Adjectives and Adverbs.**)

well-known man	a man who is well known
twelve-foot ceiling	a ceiling of twelve feet
up-to-date information	he is up to date
on-the-job training	training is on the job

There are exceptions. Some compound adjectives retain the hyphen even if they follow the word they modify. Some you should know are

All words (nouns and adjectives) that start with "self":

self-reliant boy	he is self-reliant
self-supporting girl	she is self-supporting
self-cleaning oven	it is self-cleaning

All adjective compounds that start with "all":

all-encompassing book   the book is all-encompassing

All adjectival compounds that start with "half":

half-done cake   cake was half-done
half-awake student   student was half-awake
half-explored territory   territory is only half-explored

Compound adjectives that use "ly" are not hyphenated before or after the word they modify.

highly developed muscles   his muscles were highly developed
interestingly formed rocks   rocks that are interestingly formed

In general, compound words that serve as nouns are not hyphenated. Compare:

Problem solving (noun) was his talent.

He had a *problem-solving* (adjective) talent.

Mary is a *foster child.* (noun)

She lives at the *foster-child* (adjective) home.

14.9.2 Exceptions

All "in-laws" take a hyphen.

brother-in-law   mother-in-law   sisters-in-law

In addition, hyphens have other uses, as follows:

In a series of hyphenated words with a common ending, hyphens are carried over so it is not necessary to repeat the word each time.

Is it a 100- or 200-page book?

Do you want a two-, three-, or five-column page?

They took six- and eight-cylinder cars along.

Both pro- and anti-American sentiment mounted.

Numbers from 21 to 99 are hyphenated when they are spelled out.

eighty-eight

sixty-three

two hundred forty-four

A hyphen is used to mean "up to and including" when used between numbers and dates.

1965-75   There will be 10-15 people.

the academic year 1992-93

A hyphen is also used to avoid ambiguity when two capitalized names stand together.

the Boston-New York game

the Chicago-London flight

the Kramer-Lewis debate

the Harrison-Jones marriage

Many words still have prefixes that are set off by hyphens.

pre-engineering   ex-wife *(always set "ex" off)*

pro-German   semi-independent

anti-Nixon *(prefixes added to proper nouns should always be hyphenated)*

14.10 Brackets

Brackets are probably the least used form of the pause. They do, however, serve some very useful purposes in clarifying material. When an editor needs to add corrections, explanations, or comments, brackets are used.

"They [the Murphys] never meant to send that message to the White House." (Without the bracketed words, the reader would not know who had sent the message.)

Morris continued, "After the treaty was signed [The Treaty of Versailles], jubilation filled their hearts."

The *Times* printed the senator's speech, which was addressed to "my countrymen, my countywomen [sic]." (The term [sic] indicates that the error is in the original source quoted; in this case "countywomen" should have been "countrywomen.")

Brackets are also used to avoid confusion when it is necessary to use parentheses inside of parentheses.

Darkness fell so rapidly that she and her companion (June Morrison, who had herself traveled throughout Africa [particularly Nigeria]) hardly noticed the transition from crystal blue to black.

We know of a number of scholars who disagree with this theory (see Jackson Hewitt, *To Earth's Center* [Boston: Inkwell Press, 1953], p. 614).

14.11 Ellipsis

Ellipsis (three dots:...) is used to show that words not essential to the meaning of the sentence have been omitted. A fourth dot/period is necessary when the omitted material comes at the end of a sentence.

"Fourscore and seven years ago, our fathers brought forth upon this continent a new nation,..."

"I pledge allegiance to the flag of the United States of America ...one nation under God..."

CHAPTER 15

Numbers

In writing, numbers can be either spelled out or represented by the figures themselves. Although there is no definite rule, there are some guidelines that should be followed.

15.1 Over 100 and Under 100

Most writers spell out numbers under 100 and use figures for 100 and over.

for eighteen years	306 buildings
eleven states	only 514 more cars
forty-five years old	4,762 students
ninety-nine percent	I agree 100 percent

15.1.1 Starting a Sentence

A number that starts a sentence should always be spelled out, even if it is over 100.

Three thousand forty-two voters selected Ross.

Nineteen eighty-five is a year I will never forget.

Ninety-five dollars did not seem like much to me for the hat.

15.1.2 In the Same Paragraph

Within the same paragraph, numbers that refer to the same category should be treated alike. Be consistent; be careful not to use figures for some and then spell others out.

Forty-six men and *118 women* joined the club last year. In comparison, the year before, *35 men* and *56 women* joined. (Only the number that starts the sentence is spelled out.)

15.1.3 Large Rounded Numbers

Very large numbers are usually spelled out if they are round numbers.

The earth may be *4 billion* years old.

That house supposedly sold for *$1 million*. (Do not use both "$" and "dollars," because they mean the same thing.)

Some baseball players make *$2.5 million* a year now.

> OR

Some baseball players make *2.5 million* dollars a year now.

15.2 Ordinal Numbers and Fractions

Write out ordinal numbers (fourth, twenty-third, etc.) rather than writing them as figures with letter endings.

It is usually clearer to use figures when writing a fraction.

The brochure was printed on 9-inch by 12½-inch paper.

The board for the bed was .78 of an inch too short.

When Susan was in school, she had a 3.2 average.

15.3 Addresses

Addresses are usually written in figures.

14 Mill Brook Road, Sumerset Glen, IA 23567

P.O. Box 583, Winding Ridge, Gloryville, WV 25432

200 East 50th Street, New York, NY 10022

When the numbers in the address can be spelled out in one or two words, it is also acceptable to spell them out.

One Park Avenue

Two Hundred West Lake Drive

Forty-one Fifth Avenue

Three Thousand Oaks Road

15.4 Dates

There are a number of different ways to write dates.

July 3, 1992	OR	3 July 1992
July third	OR	the third of July
nineteenth century	OR	the 1800s
the sixties	OR	the '60s

15.5 Parts of a Book

Whenever mentioning parts of a book (page numbers, sections, chapters, exercises), use figures.

Please refer to page 184 in chapter 6 of your history book if you want the answer to your question.

We found four case studies in section 8 of Jack's first-year law book.

The teacher assigned exercise 12 on page 235.

15.6 Plural Forms

To form the plural of spelled-out numbers, follow the same rules you follow to form the plural of other nouns.

They came in twos and threes.

He's in his thirties.

To form the plural of figures, add only "s."

There could never be two $8\frac{1}{2}$s.

The 1880s and the 1890s were exciting times in American history.

CHAPTER 16

Capitalization

When a letter is capitalized, it calls special attention to itself. This attention should be for a good reason. There are standard uses for capital letters as well as much difference of opinion as to what should and should not be capitalized. In general, capitalize (1) all proper nouns, (2) the first word of a sentence, and (3) the first word of a direct quotation.

16.1 Proper Nouns

All proper nouns should be capitalized. The groups below illustrate the different classifications of words that would be capitialized.

16.1.1 Names of Ships, Aircraft, Spacecraft, and Trains

Apollo 13	*Mariner IV*
DC-10	S.S. *United States*
Sputnik II	Boeing 707

16.1.2 Names of Deities

God	Jupiter
Allah	Holy Ghost
Buddha	Diana
Jehovah	Shiva

16.1.3 Geological Periods

Neolithic age   Cenozoic era
Ice Age   Tertiary period

16.1.4 Names of Astronomical Bodies

Venus   Big Dipper
the Milky Way   Halley's comet
Ursa Major   North Star
Scorpio   Deneb
the Crab nebula   Pleiades

(Note that sun, moon, and earth are not capitalized unless they are used with other astronomical terms that are capitalized.)

16.1.5 Personifications

Reliable *Nature* brought her promise of spring.
Bring on *Melancholy* in his sad might.
Morning in the bowl of night has flung the stone/That set the
  stars to flight.

16.1.6 Historical Periods

the Middle Ages   World War I
Reign of Terror   Great Depression
Christian Era   Roaring Twenties
Age of Louis XIV   Renaissance

16.1.7 Organizations, Associations, and Institutions

Girl Scouts of America   Ku Klux Klan
New York Yankees   Kiwanis Club
Smithsonian Institution   League of Women Voters

16.1.8 Government and Judicial Groups

New Jersey City Council   House of Commons
U.S. Senate   Parliament
Arkansas Supreme Court   House of Representatives

127

16.1.9 General Terms that Accompany Specific Names

A general term that accompanies a specific name is capitalized only if it follows the specific name. If it stands alone or comes before the word, it is put in lowercase.

Washington State	the state of Washington
Senator Dirksen	the senator from Illinois
Central Park	the park
Golden Gate Bridge	the bridge
President Andrew Jackson	the president of the United States

16.2 Sentences and Sentence Fragments

Use a capital to start a sentence or a sentence fragment.

Our car would not start.

When will you leave? I need to know right away.

Never!

Let me in! Right now!

16.3 Sentences within Sentences

When a sentence appears within a sentence, start it with a capital.

The main question is, Where do we start?

My sister said, "I'll find the Monopoly set."

He answered, "We can stay only a few minutes."

16.4 Lines of Poetry

In poetry, it is usual practice to capitalize the first word of each line, even if the word comes in the middle of a sentence.

She dwells with Beauty—Beauty that must die;
And Joy, whose hand is ever at his lips
Bidding Adieu.

—John Keats *16.12*

16.5 Titles of Works

The most important words of titles are capitalized. Those words not capitalized are conjunctions (e.g., *and, or, but*), articles *(a, the, an)*, and short prepositions (e.g., *of, on, by, for)*. The first and last words of a title must always be capitalized.

A Man for All Seasons	*Crime and Punishment*
Of Mice and Men	*Let Me In*
Rise of the West	"What to Look For"
Sonata in G-Minor	"The Ever-Expanding West"
Strange Life of Ivan Osokin	*Rubaiyat of Omar Khayyam*
"All in the Family"	Symphony No. 41
"Ode to Billy Joe"	Piano Concerto No. 5

CHAPTER 17

Spelling

It is important to learn to spell properly. Poor spelling is usually a sign of haste or carelessness, and it is often taken as a sign of ignorance or illiteracy. Yet learning to spell correctly is indeed more difficult for some people than for others. In any case, it can be mastered with time and patience.

There are many helpful practices to improve spelling: using the dictionary, keeping a list of words that cause difficulty, familiarizing oneself with word origin, and studying the word list and the rules in this chapter.

17.1   Word Analysis

A basic knowledge of the English language, especially familiarity with its numerous prefixes, can help build vocabulary and also strengthen spelling skills. For example, if one knows that *inter-* means *between* and that *intra-* means *within,* one is not likely to spell *intramural* as *intermural.* (The former means within the limits of a city, a college, etc.)

The following table lists some common Latin and Greek prefixes, which form part of the foundation of the English language.

PREFIX	MEANING	ENGLISH EXAMPLE
ab-, a-, abs-	away, from	abstain
ad-	to, toward	adjacent

PREFIX	MEANING	ENGLISH EXAMPLE
ante-	before	antecedent
anti-	against	antidote
bi-	two	bisect
cata-, cat-, cath-	down	cataclysm
circum-	around	circumlocution
contra-	against	contrary
de-	down, from	decline
di-	twice	diatonic
dis-, di-	apart, away	dissolve
epi-, ep-, eph-	upon, among	epidemic
ex-, e-	out of, from	extricate
hyper-	beyond, over	hyperactive
hypo-	under, down, less	hypodermic
in-	in, into	instill
inter-	among, between	intercede
intra-	within	intramural
meta-, met-	beyond, along with	metaphysics
mono-	one	monolith
non-	no, not	nonsense
ob-	against	obstruct
para-, par-	beside	parallel
per-	through	permeate
pre-	before	prehistoric
pro-	before	project
super-	above	superior
tele-, tel-	far	television
trans-	across	transpose
ultra-	beyond	ultraviolet

17.2 Spelling List

100 COMMONLY MISSPELLED WORDS

There are some words that consistently give writers trouble. The list below contains about 100 words that are commonly misspelled. In studying this list, each person will find that certain words are more troublesome than others. These in particular should be reviewed.

accommodate	February	professor
achievement	height	prominent
acquire	immediately	pursue
among	interest	quiet
apparent	its, it's	receive
arguing	led	procedure
argument	lose	profession
athletics	losing	receiving
belief	marriage	recommend
believe	mere	referring
beneficial	necessary	remember
benefited	occasion	repetition
bureau	occurred	rhythm
business	occurrence	sense
category	occurring	separate
comparative	opinion	separation
conscious	opportunity	similar
controversial	parallel	studying
define	particular	succeed
definitely	performance	succession
definition	personal	surprise
describe	personnel	technique
description	possession	than
despair	possible	their, they're, there
disastrous	practical	then
effect	precede	thorough
embarrass	prejudice	to, too, two
environment	prepare	tomorrow
exaggerate	prevalent	transferred
existence	principal	unnecessary
existent	principle	villain
experience	privilege	write
explanation	probably	writing
fascinate	proceed	

As a handy reference, it is a good idea to set aside an area in a notebook to list problem words. Add to it any new words that are persistent spelling problems.

17.3 Spelling Rules

17.3.1 Prefixes

Prefixes (such as *dis-, mis-, in-, un-,* and *re-*) are added to words without doubling or dropping letters.

dis + appear = disappear

dis + agree = disagree

dis + service = disservice

dis + solved = dissolved

dis + appoint = disappoint

dis + satisfied = dissatisfied

mis + information = misinformation

mis + spelled = misspelled

mis + understand = misunderstand

mis + led = misled

in + capable = incapable

in + definite = indefinite

in + numerable = innumerable

un + usual = unusual

un + seen = unseen

un + named = unnamed

re + elect = reelect

re + search = research

17.3.2 Suffixes

When forming adverbs from adjectives ending in *–al,* the ending becomes *–ally.*

normal	normally	real	really
occasional	occasionally	legal	legally
royal	royally		

Words ending in *n* keep the *n* when adding *–ness.*

| openness | stubbornness | suddenness | brazenness |

All words ending in *–ful* have only one *l*.

cupful	cheerful
forgetful	doleful
mouthful	graceful
helpful	meaningful
spoonful	handful

Add *–ment* without changing the root word's spelling.

adjust + ment = adjustment

develop + ment = development

amaze + ment = amazement

When a suffix beginning with a vowel is added, a word ending in a silent *e* generally drops the *e*.

Example:

admire + able = admirable

allure + ing = alluring

believe + able = believable

come + ing = coming

dare + ing = daring

deplore + able = deplorable

desire + ous = desirous

explore + ation = exploration

fame + ous = famous

imagine + able = imaginable

move + able = movable

note + able = notable

However, the word retains the *e* when a suffix beginning with a consonant is added.

Example:

arrange + ment = arrangement

glee + ful = gleeful

like + ness = likeness

134

spite + ful = spiteful

time + less = timeless

With *judgment, acknowledgment,* and other words formed by adding *–ment* to a word with a *–dge* ending, the final *e* is usually dropped, although it is equally correct to retain it.

When adding *–ous* or *–able* to a word ending in *–ge* or *–ce,* keep the final *e* when adding the suffix. The *e* is retained to keep the soft sound of the *c* or *g.*

courageous	manageable	outrageous
changeable	advantageous	traceable

17.3.3 IE + EI

In words with *ie* or *ei* in which the sound is $\bar{e}$,(long *ee*), use *i* before *e* except after *c.*

Examples: i before *e:*

believe	pier	shield	wield
chief	priest	siege	yield
niece	reprieve		

Examples: Except after *c:*

ceiling   conceit   conceive   deceive   perceive   receive

The following words are some exceptions to the rule and must be committed to memory.

either	conscience	weird	reign
leisure	height	freight	weigh
neither	forfeit	seize	neighbor

Except before *–ing,* the final *y* usually changes to *i.*

rely + ance = reliance

study + ing = studying

modify + er = modifier

modify + ing = modifying

amplify + ed = amplified

amplify + er = amplifier

amplify + ing = amplifying

When preceded by a vowel, the final *y* does not change to *i*.

annoying, annoyed

destroying, destroyed, destroyer

journeyman, journeyed, journeyer

17.3.4 Doubling the Final Consonant

In one-syllable words that end in a single consonant preceded by a single vowel, double the final consonant before adding a suffix that begins with a vowel.

drop + ing = drop(p)ing

clap + ed = clap(p)ed

man + ish = man(n)ish

snap + ed = snap(p)ed

quit + ing = quit(t)ing

However, when a suffix begins with a consonant, do not double the final consonant before adding the suffix.

man + hood = manhood

glad + ly = gladly

bad + ly = badly

fat + ness = fatness

sin + ful = sinful

This is also the case in multisyllabic words that are accented on the final syllable and have endings as described above.

admit + ed = admit(t)ed

begin + ing = begin(n)ing

commit + ed = commit(t)ed

BUT

commit + ment = commitment

However, in words with this type of ending, in which the final syllable is not accented, the final consonant is not doubled.

happen + ing = happening

profit + able = profitable

comfort + ed = comforted

refer + ence = reference

confer + ence = conference

Only three words end in *ceed* in English. They are *exceed, proceed,* and *succeed.* All other "seed-sounding" words (except *supersede*) end in *cede.*

intercede	recede
concede	accede
secede	precede

17.4 Proofreading

The best way to improve spelling is to reread what has been written. In fact, many other writing problems can be avoided as well if the writer carefully rereads and revises. Remember, poor spelling is not something that must be lived with. With a little work, it can be greatly improved.

MAXnotes®

REA's Literature Study Guides

MAXnotes® are student-friendly. They offer a fresh look at masterpieces of literature, presented in a lively and interesting fashion. **MAXnotes®** offer the essentials of what you should know about the work, including outlines, explanations and discussions of the plot, character lists, analyses, and historical context. **MAXnotes®** are designed to help you think independently about literary works by raising various issues and thought-provoking ideas and questions. Written by literary experts who currently teach the subject, **MAXnotes®** enhance your understanding and enjoyment of the work.

Available **MAXnotes®** include the following:

Absalom, Absalom!
The Aeneid of Virgil
Animal Farm
Antony and Cleopatra
As I Lay Dying
As You Like It
The Autobiography of
    Malcolm X
The Awakening
Beloved
Beowulf
Billy Budd
The Bluest Eye, A Novel
Brave New World
The Canterbury Tales
The Catcher in the Rye
The Color Purple
The Crucible
Death in Venice
Death of a Salesman
The Divine Comedy I: Inferno
Dubliners
Emma
Euripides' Medea & Electra
Frankenstein
Gone with the Wind
The Grapes of Wrath
Great Expectations
The Great Gatsby
Gulliver's Travels
Hamlet
Hard Times

Heart of Darkness
Henry IV, Part I
Henry V
The House on Mango Street
Huckleberry Finn
I Know Why the Caged
    Bird Sings
The Iliad
Invisible Man
Jane Eyre
Jazz
The Joy Luck Club
Jude the Obscure
Julius Caesar
King Lear
Les Misérables
Lord of the Flies
Macbeth
The Merchant of Venice
The Metamorphoses of Ovid
The Metamorphosis
Middlemarch
A Midsummer Night's Dream
Moby-Dick
Moll Flanders
Mrs. Dalloway
Much Ado About Nothing
My Antonia
Native Son
1984
The Odyssey
Oedipus Trilogy

Of Mice and Men
On the Road
Othello
Paradise Lost
A Passage to India
Plato's Republic
Portrait of a Lady
A Portrait of the Artist
    as a Young Man
Pride and Prejudice
A Raisin in the Sun
Richard II
Romeo and Juliet
The Scarlet Letter
Sir Gawain and the
    Green Knight
Slaughterhouse-Five
Song of Solomon
The Sound and the Fury
The Stranger
The Sun Also Rises
A Tale of Two Cities
The Taming of the Shrew
The Tempest
Tess of the D'Urbervilles
Their Eyes Were Watching God
To Kill a Mockingbird
To the Lighthouse
Twelfth Night
Uncle Tom's Cabin
Waiting for Godot
Wuthering Heights

RESEARCH & EDUCATION ASSOCIATION
61 Ethel Road W. • Piscataway, New Jersey 08854
Phone: (908) 819-8880

Please send me more information about MAXnotes®.

Name _____

Address _____

City _____ State _____ Zip_____